Ohio

Ohio

Ann Heinrichs

Children's Press®
A Division of Grolier Publishing
New York   London   Hong Kong   Sydney
Danbury, Connecticut

Frontispiece: Trees at sunset

Front cover: Snowy schoolhouse

Back cover: Cincinnati skyline

Consultant: Barbara Maslekoff, Ohioana Library

Please note: All statistics are as up-to-date as possible at the time of publication.

Visit Children's Press on the Internet at http://publishing.grolier.com

Book production by Editorial Directions, Inc.

Library of Congress Cataloging-in-Publication Data

Heinrichs, Ann.
    Ohio / Ann Heinrichs.
      144 p. 24 cm. — (America the beautiful. Second series)
    Includes bibliographical references and index.
    Summary : Describes the geography, plants, animals, history, economy, language,
religions, culture, sports, art, and people of the state of Ohio.
    ISBN 0-516-20995-7
    1. Ohio—Juvenile literature. [1. Ohio.] I. Title. II. Series.
    F491.3.H44 1999
    977.1—dc21
                                                   98-50079
                                                 CIP
                                                 AC

GROLIER
PUBLISHING

©1999 by Children's Press®, a division of Grolier Publishing Co., Inc.
All rights reserved. Published simultaneously in Canada
Printed in the United States of America
1 2 3 4 5 6 7 8 9 10 R 08 07 06 05 04 03 02 01 00 99

Acknowledgments

For their kind assistance in this project, I am grateful to innumerable employees of Ohio's state library and archives, department of development, and travel and tourism division; and to all the Ohioans who shared their experiences with me.

The Cleveland skyline

Farms in the Till Plains

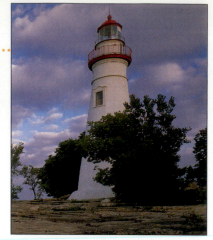

Marblehead Lighthouse

Contents

A ladybug

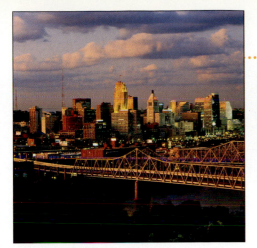

Cincinnati skyline

Ohio River

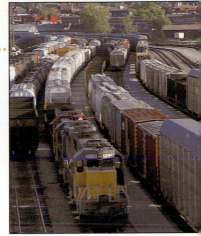

Freight trains

A cardinal

CHAPTER ONE

Built on Tradition

Samuel is up before the first rays of dawn glow in the east. He lights a lantern and slips into his white shirt, black trousers, and suspenders. In the kitchen, Samuel's mother, in her white apron and cap, prepares a hearty breakfast on the gas stove. His sister Rebecca helps with little Amos, while his father studies the Bible by lantern light. After a prayer, everyone settles down to eat.

Here at home, Samuel and his family speak a dialect of German. It's the common language among Ohio's Amish people. The people of this religious community lead a quiet, peaceful life, farming in northeastern Ohio. In keeping with their conservative beliefs, they live plainly and simply without modern conveniences.

For the Amish, children are gifts from God, and education is important. In his one-room Amish schoolhouse, Samuel studies both English and German, as well as religion and practical subjects. He and his classmates are practicing their speeches and skits for next week's program. All the parents will attend to see what their

Amish people live and work on farms.

Opposite: An Amish buggy in Holmes County

An Amish barn raising

children have learned during the school year.

After school, Samuel begins his farm chores. He leads the cows into the barn, where he and his mother do the milking. After supper it's time for homework, then an early bedtime. Tonight Samuel can hardly sleep. He's excited about the next day's barn raising.

Before daybreak, Samuel's father hitches up the horse and buggy. Samuel and Rebecca scramble into the back seat. Soon they arrive at a neighbor's farm. As the men go to work with hammers and saws, Samuel plays ball with the other children and runs errands for the carpenters. By noon, all the walls are up.

Meanwhile, the women have prepared a delicious meal to be served outdoors. After a prayer, everyone digs in. Then it's back to work. Samuel notices how quickly the work goes when everyone pitches in. By late afternoon, the roof is in place and the men put on the finishing touches. He looks with amazement on the finished product—an entire barn, completed in one day.

Ohio is one of most industrialized states in the country. Its steel, tires, cars, and aircraft are shipped to markets all over the world. Ohio is the top manufacturer of car parts in the United States. It ranks second in steel and motor vehicle production and third in the value of its manufactured goods.

In this modern, industrial state, Samuel's family and neighbors

Geopolitical map of Ohio

seem to belong to another world. Ohio's Amish people make up just a small percentage of the state's population as a whole. But their simple virtues—hard work, self-reliance, and neighborly charity—have been part of Ohio's heritage since its earliest days. Armed with these same values, Ohioans built their homeland from a frontier wilderness into the industrial giant it is today.

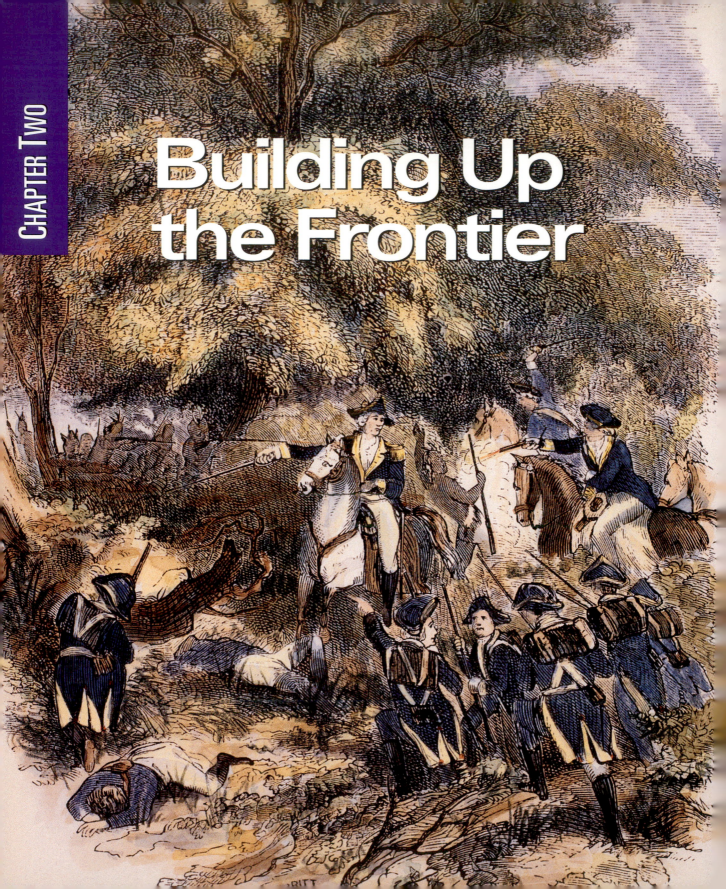

CHAPTER TWO

Building Up the Frontier

Ancient people may have lived in Ohio as early as 13,000 B.C. They arrived after the great glaciers of the Ice Age retreated. Moving in small groups, they lived by hunting wild animals and gathering herbs and nuts. Spear and arrow tips found along the Ohio River date from 7000 B.C.

Mounds at Hopewell Culture National Historic Park

In time, people began to settle in permanent camps. They made knives, axes, and tools to grind and stir their food. Some groups performed religious ceremonies or carried on trade with neighboring tribes.

More advanced people called the Mound Builders lived in Ohio beginning around 1000 B.C. They left behind more than 6,000 burial and ceremonial mounds and fortifications. Archaeologists have found two distinct ways of life among Ohio's early Mound Builders—the Adena and the Hopewell cultures.

The Adena people flourished from about 1000 B.C. to 100 B.C. They cultivated plants such as sunflowers and squash, made pottery to store food, and buried their dead in mounds. Next came the Hopewell people, who lasted until A.D. 500. Ancient Hopewell sites reveal that they made artistic ornaments and stone blades and used fire in their rituals. They traded far and wide to get seashells, copper, and mica—a mineral that can be split into thin sheets.

The Hopewell people were fabulous earth-builders. They encir-

Opposite: The Battle of Fallen Timbers

Serpent Mound

Serpent Mound is the most important prehistoric site in Ohio and the largest and best-preserved effigy mound in the United States. (An effigy mound is built to represent an animal.) Located in Adams County, the Serpent Mound looks like a winding, coiling snake 1,330 feet (405 m) long. Many mysteries surround the mound, but it seems to have had a religious or mystical purpose. The ends line up with sun's position on two days called the solstices—the longest and shortest days of the year. Other mounds nearby were built by the Adena culture, but scientists believe the Serpent Mound dates from around A.D. 1070. That would place it much later—in the era of Ohio's Fort Ancient culture. ■

cled hilltops with high earthen walls. They also built up mounds of earth into round, square, and eight-sided shapes, some covering many acres. Newark Earthworks is the largest of these sites. A long roadway called the Hopewell Road links mounds in Newark and Chillicothe—60 miles (97 km) apart. Scientists believe the road had a sacred meaning and purpose. No one is sure who lived in Ohio after the Hopewell people disappeared.

From A.D. 900 to 1600, people of the Fort Ancient culture occupied the river valleys of what is now southern Ohio. They lived in villages of several houses facing an open plaza and surrounded by a wooden fence for protection. They hunted, fished, gathered wild plants, and grew maize (corn), beans, and squash. Other Native American groups in this period were the Sandusky (northwest), Whittlesey (northeast), and Monongahela (east).

Ohio's earliest European explorers found almost no people there. The Erie tribe had lived along the lakeshore, but invading Iroquois had driven them out in the 1650s. By 1750, many Indian groups had migrated to Ohio's forests and built villages there. In

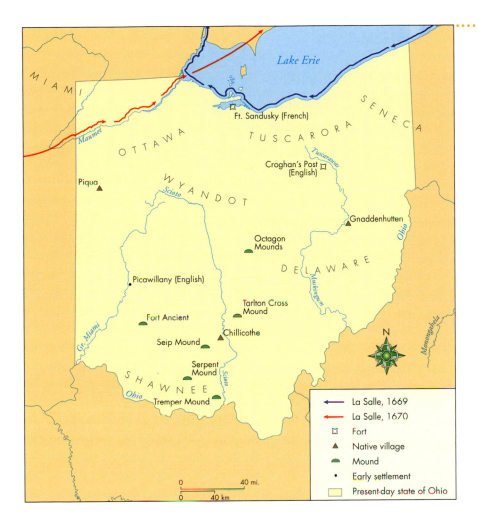

Exploration of Ohio

the northwest were the Ottawa, and remnants of the Erie lived in the north. Tribes of the Iroquois Confederacy—the Seneca, Wyandot (Huron), and Tuscarora—occupied central and northeastern Ohio. The Miami lived in what is now western Ohio, and the Shawnee lived in the south. The Delaware lived along the Muskingum River.

Fighting over the Frontier

The first European in Ohio was probably the French explorer René-Robert Cavelier, Sieur de La Salle. While he was in Canada,

René-Robert Cavelier, Sieur de La Salle

George Rogers Clark and his men fought at the Battle of Piqua during the American Revolution.

Seneca Indians had told him of a great river to the south. They called it the *Ohio*, meaning "beautiful river."

La Salle is believed to have explored the Ohio River in 1669–1670. Based on his explorations and maps, France claimed all the land north and west of the Ohio River. Another Frenchman, the explorer and fur trader Louis Jolliet, was sailing along Lake Erie's shore around the same time. Some say it was Jolliet who first reached Ohio.

England believed it had a claim to the great western wilderness, too. English colonists along the Atlantic coast thought their borders extended west into the frontier. Deep in the forests, the English and French competed for the rich fur trade. As French soldiers built forts closer and closer to the English colonies, hostilities broke out from time to time.

In 1754, these conflicts exploded into the French and Indian War. Both sides used Indians to help them fight the war. In 1763, England and France finally made peace in the Treaty of Paris. France gave Britain most of its land east of the Mississippi River, including Ohio.

War and Peace

From 1775 to 1783, the American colonies fought the British for their independence. Most of the battles of the Revolutionary War took place near the East Coast. But on the frontier, the British recruited Indians to fight on their side. In Ohio, Shawnee Indians clashed with George Rogers Clark's men at the Battle of Piqua, near Springfield. Clark's victory helped keep the territory out of British hands.

After winning its independence, the new United States promptly organized the Northwest Territory—the vast region northwest of the Ohio River. It included the present-day states of Ohio, Indiana, Illinois, Michigan, Wisconsin, and part of Minnesota.

In the Land Ordinance of 1785, Congress mapped out the way this land should be divided up for settlement. The vast territory was split into separate states. The entire area was ruled by one governor, a secretary, and three judges. Two regions of Ohio, however, were already spoken for.

"From Sea to Sea"

When the original colonies were founded, the king of England granted that their lands would extend "from sea to sea." That is, each colony would stretch like a ribbon from the Atlantic coast all the way to the Pacific. By 1786, most eastern states had simply understood that unclaimed land to the west of them also belonged to the U.S. government.

Connecticut, however, insisted on its original rights, and Congress could not untangle this legal mess. Finally, Connecticut was allowed to keep a section of northeast Ohio. It was called the

Historical map of Ohio

Western Reserve—reserved for Connecticut citizens. Some of Ohio's biggest cities were to grow up in the Western Reserve—Cleveland, Akron, Youngstown, and Sandusky. In 1800, Connecticut and the federal government agreed to make the Western Reserve part of the Ohio Territory. Virginia had a similar claim. It was granted a section of southwest Ohio as the Virginia Military District.

In 1788, Rufus Putnam gathered together a group of New Englanders called the Ohio Company of Associates and led them into the wilderness of southeast Ohio. There he founded the town of Marietta, Ohio's first permanent settlement.

The Last Indian War

Meanwhile, in the northwest, Shawnee chief Blue Jacket gathered together warriors from many tribes and organized them to resist further settlement. Legend says that Blue Jacket was a white man adopted by Indians. In any case, he struggled to protect the Indians' homeland. In 1794, General Anthony Wayne and his army of 3,000 men marched off to meet them. They met near Toledo in

Rufus Putnam

Rufus Putnam (1738–1824) served in the French and Indian War and the American Revolution, in which he was the army's chief engineer. After the war, Putnam pushed Congress to let war veterans settle in the Northwest Territory. He succeeded, and in 1786 he organized former army officers into the Ohio Company of Associates. The next year they arrived at present-day Marietta, where they established Ohio's first town. Putnam was surveyor general of the United States from 1796 to 1803. He died in Marietta. ■

the Battle of Fallen Timbers and the Indians suffered a terrible defeat.

Indian and U.S. representatives met in 1795 and agreed to the Treaty of Greenville. They drew a line across the territory: Indians were to stay to the north and west, while settlers had the south and east—about two-thirds of present-day Ohio. With the Indians' power broken at last, settlers poured into Ohio's lush river valleys.

Statehood

Ohioans hoped for statehood, but first they had to have a population of at least 5,000 adult men. Ohio took a census in 1797, and they met the quota. Now they had the right to elect a house of representatives.

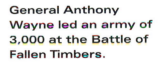

General Anthony Wayne led an army of 3,000 at the Battle of Fallen Timbers.

Ohio's first legislature met in Cincinnati in 1799. It elected William Henry Harrison to represent the Ohio Territory in the U.S. Congress. There Harrison pushed for statehood and made it easier for Ohio settlers to own land. In 1800, Congress passed a bill allowing Ohio to form its state government. At last, President Thomas Jefferson signed the statehood bill. Ohio entered the Union as the seventeenth state on March 1, 1803. Edward Tiffin was sworn in as the first governor, and Chillicothe was the first state capital.

CHAPTER THREE

A Century of Progress

Settlers making their way into Ohio

"Hi-o, away we go, floating down the river on the O-hi-o." That was the song of thousands of families on their way to the Ohio River valley. Some came from New England, where farmers could not raise huge crops of grain on their soil. Others came from Virginia and the Carolinas. They packed up their belongings, left their friends, farms, and villages behind, and headed west for the Ohio frontier.

New settlers hacked out trails through the wilderness, cut down trees to make clearings, and built log cabins. The cabins had two or three rooms, a fireplace and chimney for cooking, and maybe even glass windowpanes. The whole family pitched in with chores. They tended cattle, hogs, and chickens and raised grain, vegetables, and fruit. Women and girls cooked, baked bread and pies, and made candles, soap, and clothes. In the forest, men and their sons hunted deer and wild turkeys and found golden honey in bee trees.

Neighbors lived miles apart, but they pitched in for barn raisings. While the men labored, the women served food and drinks. When the work was done, it was time to relax, sing, and dance. Simple churches went up too. The preachers were circuit riders, traveling from one church to another on the frontier. Pioneers often met new neighbors at church services. They traded news, gos-

Opposite: The Battle of Lake Erie

sip, recipes, and crop stories. Church was also a good place for young men and women to find marriage partners.

After the pioneers came doctors, blacksmiths, storekeepers, and schoolteachers. In one-room, red-brick schoolhouses, pioneer children learned the three Rs—reading, writing, and 'rithmetic.

Steamboat's a-Comin'!

One day in 1811, farmers by the Ohio River shaded their eyes and squinted to make sure they were seeing right. Down the river chugged a side-wheeled steamboat, the *New Orleans*. Billows of smoke from its wood-burning boiler poured out of its smokestack.

The steam-powered boat must have seemed an odd contraption to farmers who did their work by hand. But it was only the first of many steamers to go down the Ohio to the Mississippi River and on to New Orleans. Soon Ohio farmers were shipping their pork, flour, cheese, and other farm products down to New Orleans or upriver to Pittsburgh.

The War of 1812

For years, British ships had been stopping U.S. ships on the high seas. Officers came aboard and seized sailors they believed to be Englishmen. The British possessed Canada at the time. They had been helping Indians who resisted settlers moving into their hunting grounds. With British support, tribes in Canada and the Northwest Territory rallied under Shawnee chief Tecumseh and his brother, the Shawnee Prophet.

General William Henry Harrison marched an army into Indian territory in 1811. As the troops camped on Tippecanoe Creek in

Tecumseh and the Prophet

Tecumseh (1768?–1813) (right) was born near present-day Springfield, the son of a Shawnee chief and a Creek-Cherokee woman. In 1805, Tecumseh's brother Tenskwatawa, called the Shawnee Prophet (1778–1837), began preaching to Indians around Greenville.

Tecumseh took this chance to organize resistance against white settlers. Soon the British began to provide the brothers with supplies. The Prophet clashed with U.S. Army general William Henry Harrison in the 1811 Battle of Tippecanoe. In the War of 1812, the British made Tecumseh a brigadier general. He lost his life in the Battle of the Thames in Canada in 1813. ■

Indiana, the Prophet led a surprise attack, and Harrison's men fought them off. Harrison became a hero and acquired the nickname Old Tippecanoe, or just Old Tip for short. No one was surprised that British weapons were found on some of the dead Indians. In 1812, Congress declared war against Britain.

For Ohioans, the war came close to home. With British Canada just across the Great Lakes, many conflicts took place around Lake Erie, including the Battle of Lake Erie. In 1813, Commodore Oliver H. Perry set sail from Ohio's lakeshore. In a valiant naval battle, Perry won control of Lake Erie from the British. He reported the outcome in a now-famous message: "We have met the enemy and they are ours."

Perry's victory cleared Lake Erie for General William Henry Harrison. Harrison

William Henry Harrison

had defended Ohio's Fort Meigs from British attack. Now he went on to take Detroit back from the British. Then he crossed Lake Erie into Canada and defeated British forces at the Thames River. One victim of the battle was a warrior Harrison knew well—Chief Tecumseh. After the Battle of the Thames, Ohio was safe from British attack. The war ended in 1815 with a U.S. victory.

Roads, Canals, and Railroads

After the war, Ohio quickly expanded its industry and trade. More settlers poured in, too. By 1820, the population had risen to more than 581,000 people. Transportation was the key to this growth. The country was building its first National Road, and the Ohio segment was completed in 1838. Settlers heading west no longer had to hack out their own trails.

But canals made a bigger difference for farmers with goods to sell. The Ohio and Erie Canal, opened in 1832, ran the whole north-south length of Ohio. It connected Cleveland on Lake Erie to Portsmouth on the Ohio River. By the 1840s, dozens of locks sped up river traffic on the Muskingum River. Ohio's Miami and Erie Canal opened in 1845.

Railroads were the next novelty. The Erie and Kalamazoo Railroad between Toledo and Michigan opened in 1836. Ohio's first rail line within the state began running between Dayton and Sandusky in 1850. Coal mining

A wagon train on the National Road

Canals

Canals were gigantic "ditches" that carried boats over hilly, uneven terrain. Watercraft could actually sail uphill and downhill. Wherever the land level changed, a huge wall called a lock—like a dam—kept the water level even. While a canal boat waited behind the lock, massive pumps forced the water from one side of the lock to the other until the water level was even on both sides. Then the wall was lowered and the boat passed through smoothly. Goods were often shipped on flat canal boats called barges. Barges had no engines. Instead, they were attached by ropes to mules that trudged along the shore. ■

expanded as railroads transported tons of coal to markets. Railroads also made it profitable to farm in far-western Ohio.

Slavery, Women's Rights, and the Civil War

In the 1850s, the issue of slavery threatened to tear the United States in two. Many Northerners were abolitionists—people who wanted slavery outlawed. Meanwhile, many Southerners wanted to keep using slaves to work their plantations. Ohio was ahead of most of the nation in 1848 when it repealed its Black Laws, which denied basic civil rights to blacks. Ohio abolitionists also helped escaped slaves to cross the Ohio River and make their way to Lake Erie and freedom in Canada. This secret network was called the Underground Railroad. A stagecoach stop in Painesville called Rider's Inn became one of the stations on the secret route.

Many abolitionists believed that slavery was wrong because all people are equal. The idea of equality was also behind the women's rights movement. Ohio women were active in the cause. In 1851, a Woman's Rights Convention was held in Akron. The hottest topic was women's right to vote. But the statewide conference also included reports on education, labor, and other issues of the day.

In 1853, a National Woman's Rights Convention was held in Cleveland. Members discussed many of the problems facing women at the time. Besides the voting issue, they dealt with equal

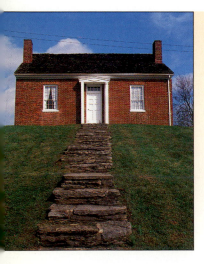

The Rankin House

The Rankin House on Liberty Hill in Ripley was a famous stop on the Underground Railroad. Here, more than 2,000 escaped slaves climbed the "stairway to freedom"—a steep, wooden staircase from the riverbank to the house. John Rankin was a Presbyterian minister devoted to the antislavery movement. From 1825 to 1865, he and his wife provided food and shelter to slaves who had escaped across the Ohio River, sometimes hiding as many as twelve at one time. In this house, it's said that Harriet Beecher Stowe heard about the slave Eliza's escape across the icy river. Later she recounted the tale in *Uncle Tom's Cabin*. The Rankin House is now a national historic landmark. ■

access to education and jobs, reform of marriage and divorce laws, and prohibition of liquor.

In 1861, the North–South conflict exploded into the Civil War. About 345,000 Ohio volunteers—twice the required quota—marched off to fight in the Union army. Some soldiers served under famous generals from their home state—Ulysses S. Grant, William Tecumseh Sherman, and Philip Sheridan.

Ohioans held high posts in President Abraham Lincoln's cabinet, too. Edwin Stanton was his secretary of war, and Salmon P. Chase was secretary of the treasury. Not everyone in Ohio believed in the Northern cause, though. Some, called copperheads, opposed the war or even sided with the South. Many of them lived in southern Ohio, near the Kentucky border.

Ulysses S. Grant served as a Union general.

Morgan's Raid

The war reached its northernmost point when it spilled into Ohio in 1863. With Union troops in hot pursuit, Confederate general John Hunt Morgan led his cavalrymen—Morgan's Raiders—on an "invasion" of southwest Ohio. It wasn't really a military mission. The raiders tore through the countryside, robbing farmhouses and looting stores. They took food, water, horses, cash—and even clocks, birdcages, and bolts of cloth.

General Morgan took pride in being a gentleman, however. One day, two girls were riding their horses along a road when they met

Ohio was the victim of Morgan's Raiders during the Civil War.

up with Morgan and his men. Knowing these were the thieving raiders, the girls dismounted, ready to be robbed of their horses. But Morgan left them alone. "Southern gentlemen don't steal ladies' horses," he said.

On another occasion, Morgan was robbing a county treasury. As he emptied the safe of its cash, he saw a pile of pretty bags. "What are those?" he asked. The treasurer replied, "They are purses of money placed here by several widowed ladies for safe-keeping." "Keep them safe," Morgan declared as he dashed out the door. "I never robbed a widow yet." Eventually, Morgan was jailed for horse thievery. He escaped, only to be killed in a surprise Union raid in Tennessee.

An Industrial Power

By the time the war was over, Ohio was far more than just a frontier farming state. Factories and steel mills had been built to meet the need for war supplies. Cities grew up quickly around the industrial sites, and railroad lines crisscrossed the state.

By 1880, with almost 3.2 million residents, Ohio was the third-largest state in America. Only New York and Pennsylvania had more residents. Ohio was quickly becoming a major industrial power, producing steel, glass, rubber, ceramics, and other manufactured goods.

New inventions were making life easier and more exciting for Ohioans. Samuel Morse invented the telegraph, and telegraph wires strung on high poles carried messages across Ohio and far beyond. Alexander Graham Bell's new invention, the telephone, ushered in a new age of communication.

Ohio's own Thomas Edison changed the world forever when he perfected the electric lightbulb. Edison also brought music into people's homes with his newfangled phonograph. James Ritty of Dayton invented a "mechanical money drawer" that rang a bell when it opened. People laughed at the device, but Ritty's enterprise became the National Cash Register Company.

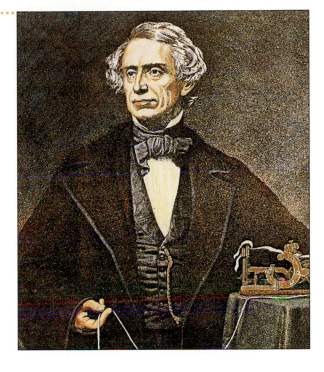

Samuel Morse was famous for his invention of the telegraph.

Thomas Edison

Thomas Alva Edison (1847–1931) was one of the most brilliant inventors of all time. Born in Milan, he spent his childhood tinkering with gadgets to figure out how they worked. His many inventions include the first practical electric lightbulb, the phonograph and record, the movie camera, the stock market's ticker tape, and the vacuum tube that made radios work. Edison often reminded his admirers that "genius is 2 percent inspiration and 98 percent perspiration." ■

Ohioans Take Charge!

As an industrial state, Ohio was a leader in organizing labor unions and improving working conditions. Workers in Ohio formed the American Federation of Labor (AFL) in 1886 and the United Mine-Workers of America in 1890. Ohio was among the first states to pass a law limiting the workday to ten hours.

When workers felt management was unfair, they sometimes took matters into their own hands. They went on strike, refusing to work until their demands were met. Railroad workers went on strike in 1877. When coal miners in the Hocking district went on strike in 1884, they set several mines on fire. To this day, the coal in those mines is still burning.

Ohio became powerful on the nation's political scene, too. From 1869 to 1881, three Ohioans in a row were president of the United States—Ulysses S. Grant (1869–1877), Rutherford B. Hayes (1877–1881), and James A. Garfield (1881). Another Ohioan, Benjamin Harrison, went to the White House in 1889. Three more Ohioans would rise to the presidency in the next few decades. With more native presidents than any other state in the Union besides Virginia, Ohio came to be known as the Mother of Presidents.

The United Mine-Workers of America was a strong force in Ohio.

Ohio Presidents in the 1800s

William Henry Harrison (1773–1841) served as the ninth president of the United States in 1841. Born in Virginia, he settled in North Bend, where he lived when he was elected president. Harrison made his name as a military hero in the Indian wars and the War of 1812. His treaty with the Indians made the Northwest Territory safe for settlement. Harrison was the first president to die in office.

Ulysses S. Grant (1822–1885), born in Point Pleasant, served as the eighteenth president from 1869 to 1877. As a brilliant Civil War general, he won many important victories and became commander of all the Union forces. He accepted Confederate general Robert E. Lee's surrender in 1865. As president, Grant was neither skillful nor wise, and his administration was wracked with corruption. However, Grant himself was not involved in any wrongdoing.

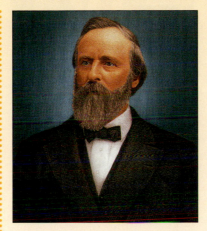

Rutherford B. Hayes (1822–1893) (above) served as the nineteenth president from 1877 to 1881. Born in Delaware, Ohio, he became a lawyer and practiced in Cincinnati. He represented Ohio as a congressman and served two terms as Ohio's governor. As president, Hayes ended Reconstruction, the period after the Civil War when the South rebuilt itself, when he pulled federal troops out of state governments. He also began reforming the nation's civil service— the government job system.

James Abram Garfield (1831–1881) served as the twentieth president in 1881. Born near Orange, he attended a Disciples of Christ school—the Eclectic Institute—and later became its principal. Garfield served in Congress for seventeen years. There he worked to improve education and protect U.S. industries from foreign competition. Four months after Garfield took office as president, an assassin shot him. He died two months later.

Benjamin Harrison (1833–1901) served as the twenty-third president from 1889 to 1893. Born in North Bend, he was the grandson of President William Henry Harrison. He became a successful lawyer in Indianapolis and a hero in the Civil War. As a U.S. senator from Indiana, Harrison favored civil service reform, civil rights, and high import taxes to protect U.S. industry. He continued these efforts as president and pushed through many important laws in these areas. ■

CHAPTER FOUR

The Modern State

At the turn of the century, Ohio turned over a new leaf. Corrupt political bosses had been running the city governments in Cincinnati, Cleveland, Toledo, and other cities. George Cox ran Cincinnati, while in Cleveland, Marcus Hanna was boss. Both were millionaires working to protect their own wealth. They were so powerful that no state official was elected without their nod of approval.

Into this mess marched two crusaders—writers Lincoln Steffens and Ida Tarbell. They were called muckrakers because they dug up so much dirt on crooked officials. Under Boss Cox, the muckrakers said, Cincinnati was the "most corrupt and worst-governed city in the country." Steffens and Tarbell exposed one outrage after another until voters were more than ready to clean up. Newly elected mayors turned their cities into shining models of good government.

Marcus Hanna had great influence in Cleveland.

Tragedies and Triumphs

Another Ohioan occupied the White House as the new century dawned. Governor William McKinley was elected president in 1896. Although McKinley may have won solely because of Marcus Hanna's masterful campaign strategies, McKinley was a good president and won reelection in 1900. The next summer, he traveled to Buffalo, New York, to give a speech at the Pan-American Exposition. "Let us ever remember that our interest is in concord, not

Opposite: The Cleveland skyline

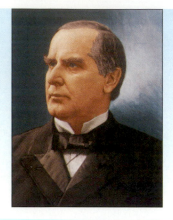

William McKinley

William McKinley (1843–1901), born in Niles, served as the twenty-fifth president from 1896 to 1901. As a congressman for fourteen years, McKinley worked to reform the way government jobs were given out. As president, he was strong in foreign affairs. He urged the building of the Panama Canal, quickly ended the Spanish-American War, and brought order to the Philippines and other former Spanish holdings. In 1901, McKinley was assassinated while attending the Pan-American Exposition in Buffalo, New York. ■

conflict," he said, emphasizing the importance of foreign trade. "And that our real eminence rests in the victories of peace, not those of war." As McKinley shook hands with admirers, a man named Leon Czolgosz broke through the crowd and shot him point-blank. Eight days later, the president was dead.

Meanwhile, in Dayton, two young men were losing interest in their bicycle-repair shop. Orville and Wilbur Wright had been hooked on flying since they were boys. They were fascinated with a toy helicopter that "flew" with rubber bands.

Orville (left) and Wilbur Wright at their home in Dayton

Certain that they could crack the mysteries of flight, they experimented with kites and gliders. In the dusty stacks of Dayton's public library, they read everything they could find about aerodynamics. It all paid off. In 1903, Orville and Wilbur hauled their flying machine to Kitty Hawk, North Carolina. The brothers took turns at it, and on the fourth try, Wilbur flew the world's first motor-powered airplane 852 feet (260 m) in 59 seconds. In 1908, the U.S. War Department signed up the Wright brothers to design airplanes for the army.

William Howard Taft

William Howard Taft (1857–1930), born in Cincinnati, served as the twenty-seventh president from 1909 to 1913. Taft enjoyed playing baseball and football at Yale University. He became a federal judge and dean of the Cincinnati Law School. In 1904, President Theodore Roosevelt appointed him secretary of war. As president, Taft aggressively attacked powerful business monopolies and fought for the conservation of natural resources. After serving one term as president of the United States, Taft went back to Yale as a law professor. Only later did he hold a position that he truly loved—chief justice of the U.S. Supreme Court (1921–1930). ■

The Floods

It was a Thursday when the rain began to fall. The next Tuesday morning—March 25, 1913—the Miami River heaved over its levees and surged through Dayton. The rushing current ripped whole houses from their foundations and carried them away. Floodwaters rose to the second-story windows of the houses that remained, while terrified residents clung to the rooftops. By the time the waters receded three days later, more than 350 people were dead.

The state legislature quickly passed the Conservancy Act for statewide flood protection. Under this plan, dams and reservoirs were built to protect Ohio's flood-prone river valleys. This was the nation's first flood-control method that targeted entire river systems.

Wartime Ohio

When the United States entered World War I in 1917, about 250,000 Ohioans joined the fight. Soldiers drilled at Camp Sherman, and pilots trained at Dayton's Fairfield Air Depot. Airman Eddie Rickenbacker of Columbus shot down more enemy aircraft than any other pilot in that war.

Charles Kettering

Charles F. Kettering (1876–1958) was born in Loudonville. Early in his career, he invented the electric cash register and the automobile battery. Until then, people started their cars with a dangerous hand crank. General Motors bought Kettering's company, Delco, and made him director of research. There he invented shock absorbers, a new kind of transmission, better headlights, and ethyl gasoline. Kettering's inventions made him wealthy, and he was generous with his money. He cofounded the Sloan-Kettering Institute for Cancer Research. When praised for his scientific talents, Kettering liked to say, "I'm a pliers and screwdriver man, not a theory man." ■

Ohioans produced tons of equipment for the war effort. Airplanes came from Dayton, steel from Cleveland and Youngstown, and rubber tires from Akron. Trucks, tanks, and precision tools rolled off the assembly lines. Thousands of people poured into the state for factory jobs.

Benjamin F. Goodrich had opened Ohio's first rubber factory in Akron in 1870. By now, many other rubber giants had joined the scene. Another booming business was automobile parts. Charles F. Kettering of Dayton invented the "automobile self-starter," better known as a battery. With a partner, Kettering founded a company called Delco (Dayton Engineering Laboratories Company).

The Ohio Gang

What a choice Ohioans had to make in 1920! Both candidates for U.S. president were Ohio's native sons. One was Republican Warren G. Harding, a U.S. senator from Marion. Running against him was Ohio's own governor, Democrat James M. Cox.

The 1920 election had an exciting new twist too. It was the first national election in which women were allowed to vote. That meant 25 million more citizens were able to voice their opinions at the polls.

Ohioans had cast their votes for Democrat Woodrow Wilson in 1912 and 1916, but in 1920 they switched their loyalties—and so did the rest of the nation. Everyone seemed to be tired of wartime issues and uncomfortable with Wilson's international policies. The result? Harding won by a landslide.

As president, Harding established a badly needed system for managing the country's income and spending. He also opened federal jobs to African-Americans for the first time. He appointed former president William Howard Taft as chief justice of the Supreme Court. But Harding came under fire for giving special favors to his poker-playing friends and political allies. Newspapers called his band of cronies the Ohio Gang. One scandal after another blackened Harding's term in office, and he died in 1923 before his term was over.

Warren G. Harding

Warren Gamaliel Harding (1865–1923) served as the twenty-ninth president from 1921 to 1923. He was born near Corsica (now Blooming Grove). Harding served six years in the U.S. Senate and was a popular public speaker.

As president, Harding negotiated naval treaties with several foreign countries. He enjoyed playing poker with his friends and appointed many of them to high government posts. This led to several national scandals, and Harding's presidency is remembered for its corruption. He died on a speaking tour before his term was over. ■

Eliot Ness

Eliot Ness (1903–1957) was a legendary crime fighter. Born in Chicago, he joined the Justice Department as a special agent to investigate gangster Al Capone. His nine-man team was nicknamed the Untouchables because they could not be bribed or frightened by mobsters. Once Capone was safely in jail, Ness set his sights on cleaning up Cleveland. As the city's director of public safety from 1935 to 1942, Ness cleaned up corruption among city officials, labor leaders, and the police department. ■

The Great Depression

The whole nation fell on hard times in the Great Depression of the 1930s. For Ohioans, life was bitterly hard. Food prices dropped, and families who had worked their land for generations had to give up their farms. People in the cities were no better off. One factory after another closed, leaving thousands of workers with no way to make a living. Fortunately, the federal government stepped in with programs that put people to work. One project built dams to control flooding in the Muskingum River valley.

Another War—and Peacetime Progress

More than 800,000 Ohioans marched off to fight in World War II (1939–1945). Across the state, military camps opened to train fighting forces. Ohioans who stayed home—both women and men—found themselves immersed in the war effort too. They rolled up their sleeves and worked long hours in factories to produce tires, steel, aircraft, ships, and ammunition. By the time the war was over, Ohio had become one of the nation's leading industrial giants.

In 1959, the St. Lawrence Seaway opened to ship traffic between the Atlantic Ocean and the Great Lakes. Eight of Ohio's ports on Lake Erie became international ports. Now Ohio could "skip the middleman" and export its goods directly to foreign countries. Within ten years, the value of Ohio's exports ranked fourth among the states.

A Time of Turmoil

In the late 1960s, college students around the country began to protest the Vietnam War. In 1970, student demonstrations at Ohio's Kent State University got so out of hand that the governor called out the National Guard to keep order. In a frenzied confrontation, guardsmen opened fire, killing four students.

Students trying to escape tear gas at Kent State University in 1970

In the 1970s, Ohio's public schools began to run short of money. Some districts even had to close their schools. To raise funds for education, the state adopted an income tax and began holding a state lottery. The 1970s were bad years for many of Ohio's factories, too. When fuel prices rose across the nation, many factories had to cut production or close down.

Modern Issues and Concerns

Today, Ohioans face many of the same challenges that other states do. People in the inner cities need more social services and better housing and living conditions. Ohio's industries are great for the economy, but they bring problems, too.

Factory wastes have caused environmental hazards and polluted Ohio's precious waterways. By the early 1990s, Lake Erie and many rivers throughout the state were badly polluted. Besides creating health problems, the murky waters were keeping people from boating, skiing, and fishing.

Ohio also faces the serious problem of foreign competition. In the 1980s, foreign steel companies appeared on the market selling steel at low prices. This forced many of Ohio's steel companies to move to states where laborers would work for lower wages. Some companies closed down altogether, leaving thousands of people without jobs.

Ohioans are now working to reverse the damage of past water and air pollution. They have passed new regulations for factories so that the state can enjoy a "cleaner" future. In the 1980s, researchers discovered ways to burn coal so that it releases very little sulfur.

In 1993, voters agreed to spend millions of their tax dollars to give their parks and recreation areas a facelift. New programs are also rebuilding the inner cities and lending a hand to Ohio's poor, both in the cities and in rural areas. As Ohio looks forward to its 200th birthday in 2003, many would say that the state is readying itself for a more prosperous future.

CHAPTER FIVE

The Land and Its Creatures

Imagine a diagonal line cutting across Ohio from northeast to southwest. That line is where two of the nation's major land regions meet. North of the line are the Central Plains; south of the line is the Appalachian region.

Farms are plentiful in Ohio's Till Plains.

Carving Out Ohio

Glaciers—massive sheets of ice—inched across Ohio during the Ice Age. They flattened out northern and western Ohio, leaving plains of rich soil behind. This half of the state is divided into two main regions—the Till Plains of western Ohio and the Great Lakes Plains of northwest Ohio and the shores of Lake Erie.

The Till Plains are part of America's vast Corn Belt. Farmers here raise corn and other grains, soybeans, and cattle. Cincinnati, Dayton, and Columbus, the state capital, are the major cities in this region.

Opposite: Old Man's Cave State Park

Putting Ohio in Its Place

Ohio is one of the nation's midwestern states. To the north are Michigan and Lake Erie, with Canada lying just across the lake. (The Ohio-Canada border actually runs through Lake Erie.) To the west is Indiana. On the southwest, across the Ohio River, is Kentucky. West Virginia borders Ohio across the river on the southeast, and Pennsylvania lies directly to the east.

The Great Lakes Plains are fertile lowlands where fruits and vegetables thrive. Some of Ohio's most important industrial cities grew up here, too, as factory towns and shipping centers on Lake Erie. They include Toledo, Sandusky, and Cleveland.

East and southeast Ohio is hilly and rough. It's part of the Appalachian Plateau that continues on to the east. This region was never flattened out during the Ice Age because glaciers did not reach that far into Ohio. Much of this area is natural and wild, with beautiful mountain scenery, dense forests, and cascading waterfalls.

A small section of south-central Ohio is called the bluegrass region. This grassy expanse of gently rolling hills is the northern end of Kentucky's bluegrass territory.

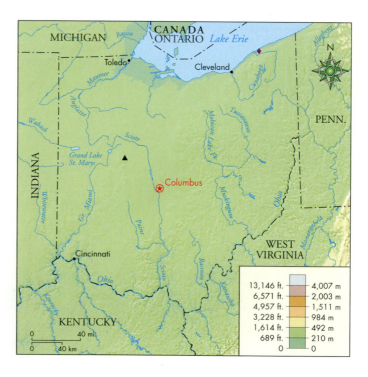

Ohio's topography

The Cuyahoga Valley

Cuyahoga Valley National Recreation Area covers about 33,000 acres (13,355 ha) between Cleveland and Akron. It surrounds the winding Cuyahoga River, which Indians called *Ka-ih-ohg-ha* (Crooked River).

The valley is a region of deep forests, rolling hills, and open farmland dotted with historic homes, old barns, and canal spillways. Hiking, biking, and horseback-riding trails meander through the valley.

In the winter, it's a great place for skiing, sledding, snowshoeing, and ice-skating. A scenic railroad takes passengers through the forest scenery to historic villages and canal towns. ■

Wild Ohio

Most of Ohio's wild animals are small. White-tailed deer are the largest. People spot them all over the state, but most live in the southeastern forests.

Rabbits, opossums, squirrels, red foxes, woodchucks, and skunks scurry around in the fields and woods. Beavers disap-

Rabbits are common in Ohio's woods.

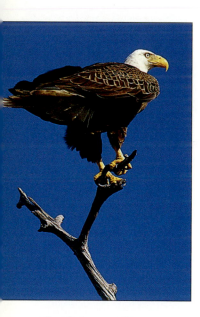

The bald eagle can sometimes be spotted in Ohio's skies.

peared from Ohio for a hundred years, but now they range over two-thirds of the state.

Feathered Friends

Wild turkeys made a hearty feast for Ohio's pioneers but, by 1904, the turkeys were gone. Too much hunting and too little forestland did them in. Starting in 1956, wildlife managers brought wild turkeys in from other states and "transplanted" them in Ohio. Now, more than 95,000 wild turkeys strut around the state.

Many other game birds find shelter in Ohio's forests, including quail, pheasants, partridges, and ruffed grouse. Meadows and open woodlands are home to swallows, meadowlarks, sparrows, thrushes, robins, and cardinals.

Among Ohio's twenty-two endangered animals, many are birds. They include bald eagles, peregrine falcons, and piping plovers. Bald eagles have made a dramatic comeback, however. In 1979, only four breeding pairs were identified in Ohio. By 1994, the population had risen to twenty-six breeding pairs.

Some birds, while not yet endangered, are becoming scarce. They include sandpipers, bobolinks, meadowlarks, and some sparrow species. However, waterbirds such as Canada geese have been increasing in numbers.

Buckeyes and Other Trees

Indians knew of the slightly smelly tree that shaded the riverbanks. They called its nut *hetuck,* meaning "eye of the buck," because of its circular markings. A botanist spied the tree on the bank of the Ohio River and named it the Ohio buckeye. That gave

Ohio its nickname—the Buckeye State. Some people call the tree "stinking buckeye" because its flowers and wood have an unpleasant smell.

Sycamore trees are the largest hardwood trees in the United States, and Ohio has plenty of them. (Hardwoods lose their leaves in the fall, while softwoods, or evergreens, don't.) The world's biggest sycamore tree stands in Jeromesville. This gigantic sycamore looms 129 feet (39 m) high, its crown spreads 105 feet (32 m), and its trunk measures 48.5 feet (14.8 m) around.

The dense hardwood forests that once covered most of Ohio were gradually cleared by settlers. Still, Ohio's forestland has more than doubled since 1940—from 3.2 million acres to 7.9 million acres (1.3 million to 3.2 million ha).

Today, forests cover about one-fourth of the state, and most trees are still hardwoods. They include beeches, maples, oaks, poplars, and ash, as well as nut trees such as hickory and walnut. Evergreen pines thrive in the hills and valleys of the southeast, where the state's thickest forests grow.

Red maples at Yellow Creek

Blooms Galore

In the springtime, Ohio's meadows and hillsides are ablaze with colorful wildflowers. There are purple bergamot and crown vetch, yellow coreopsis and black-eyed Susans, red-and-yellow Indian

Purple coneflowers and yellow black-eyed Susans

blankets, purple and yellow coneflowers, creamy cosmos, and multicolored larkspurs.

Pink prairie roses climb through thickets and shrubs, while white water lilies float on the lakes and ponds. Hummingbirds draw nectar from brilliant red cardinal flowers, and monarch butterfly caterpillars feast on the leaves of butterfly weed. Every spring, the Ohio Department of Transportation plants thousands of wildflowers along the state's highways.

Lake Erie

Lake Erie is the shallowest of the five Great Lakes. Violent storms can rise on the lake in a flash, and high waves have sent many a ship to its grave. Along with the other Great Lakes—all of which are connected—Lake Erie straddles the border between the United States and Canada. Erie is the fourth largest of them all—only Lake Ontario is smaller. However, Lake Erie is Ohio's largest body of water. It covers most of the state's northern border, stretching from Toledo eastward to Buffalo, New York.

Over the years, Lake Erie's shoreline has been eroding, or washing away. This not only makes the lake water murky and unfit for fishing and vacationers, but it also washes away property. In some spots, the shore has moved inland more than 1,000 feet (305 m) in the last hundred years.

Industrial pollution has taken its toll, too. By the late 1960s, Lake Erie was the dirtiest of the Great Lakes. Cleanups began—on both the Canadian and the Ohio sides—in the 1970s. In the 1990s, the state launched a massive project to beautify Lake Erie and freshen its waters for both people and animals.

The Marblehead Light-house on Lake Erie

Inland Waterways and Wetlands

Inland, Ohio's largest lake is Grand Lake. It was one of many lakes created artificially in the canal days. Dams were built on

Ohio's parks and forests

creeks and streams, and the backed-up water poured into the state's canals. Ohio's natural lakes fill giant pockets gouged out by ancient glaciers. More than twenty of them cover 40 acres (16 ha) or more.

The Ohio River got its name long before the land did. Seneca Indians of the Iroquois Confederation called it *Ohio*, meaning "beautiful river." It's the major eastern tributary of the Mississippi River, beginning in Pittsburgh, Pennsylvania, and entering the Mississippi at Cairo, Illinois.

The Scioto River is the Ohio's longest tributary. It flows southward into the Ohio, as do the Muskingum, Hocking, and Miami Rivers. In the north, the Maumee River empties into Lake Erie.

Many of Ohio's major cities grew up on the banks of its rivers. In the past, floods washed out the river towns routinely, but now more than 60,000 dams control the flow of the state's rivers.

Big Darby Creek and Little Darby Creek have been declared national scenic rivers. They hold eighty-six species of fish and forty types of freshwater mussels. The Nature Conservancy named the Darby Creeks' watershed one of the Last Great Places.

Ohio once had 7 million acres (2.8 million ha) of wetlands, but only about 10 percent of these marshes and swamps remain. Most are in the northern third of the state. Ohio ranks second in the United States in percent of wetlands lost to development from the 1780s to the 1980s.

The Ohio River is a tributary of the Mississippi River.

Ohio's Geographical Features

Total area; rank	44,828 sq. mi. (116,105 sq km); 35th
Land area; rank	40,953 sq. mi. (106,068 sq km); 35th
Water area; rank	3,875 sq. mi. (10,036 sq km); 11th
Inland water; rank	376 sq. mi. (974 sq km); 37th
Great Lakes water; rank	3,499 sq. mi. (9,062 sq km); 4th
Geographic center	Delaware, 25 miles (40 km) north-northeast of Columbus
Highest point	Campbell Hill, 1,550 feet (472 m)
Lowest point	Ohio River, 433 feet (132 m)
Largest city	Columbus
Population; rank	10,887,325 (1990 census); 7th
Record high temperature	113°F (45°C) near Gallipolis on July 21,1934
Record low temperature	–39°F (–39 °C) at Milligan on February 10, 1899
Average July temperature	73°F (23°C)
Average January temperature	28°F (–2°C)
Average annual precipitation	38 inches (97 cm)

Ohio's Seasons

Across Ohio, autumn leaves turn vivid crimson and gold. Visitors come from far away to take scenic drives through the fall foliage. Rural towns hold autumn harvest festivals, with pumpkins, apple cider, and other fall products.

Ohio's winters are cold and dry, thanks to the cold fronts that sweep down from Canada. Warm air over Lake Erie usually protects the lakeshore from extreme cold. Vegetable and fruit farmers in the north don't have to worry about frosts destroying their crops. But it's quite a different story in the southeastern Appalachian hills. Frosts in late spring and early fall cut the growing season short.

Summers are hot and humid, as balmy air pushes up from the Gulf of Mexico. When the Canadian and Gulf fronts collide, they cause much of Ohio's rain and snow.

Southwestern Ohio gets the heaviest rainfalls. Far-southwestern Wilmington receives about 44 inches (112 cm) every year—higher than the state's average. In Cincinnati—a city of hills—heavy rain and snow sometimes cause landslides that destroy buildings, roads, and power lines. Cincinnati has one of the nation's highest rates of landslide damage. State and federal agencies are working on ways to cut down on the damage.

Ohio's snowiest region is the northeast. About 29 inches (74 cm) of snow fall on the state as a whole, but the northeast gets around 100 inches (254 cm)—more than three times the state average. That makes the northeast a popular spot for skiing, sledding, and other winter fun.

Ohio's abundant snowfalls make sledding a popular pastime.

CHAPTER SIX

Touring Ohio

Columbus, on the banks of the Scioto River, is Ohio's capital. It's one of the fastest-growing cities in the nation, with more than 150 high-tech companies headquartered there. But Columbus offers much more than modern high-rise buildings. It's a city of century-old homes, lively neighborhoods, a large university, and a famous zoo.

Columbus is a large, fast-growing city.

Columbus is the largest city in the world that's named after Christopher Columbus. In 1992, the city celebrated the 500th anniversary of Columbus's arrival in the New World. A full-sized replica of his flagship the *Santa Maria* is docked on the Scioto River downtown.

The Ohio Historical Center highlights prehistoric people and their arts and way of life. The center's Ohio Village is a rural town complete with costumed residents who recreate Ohio's pioneer days.

Columbus's Center of Science and Industry (COSI) is a hands-on science museum for young people. Its four floors of exhibits include a planetarium and the Game of Hearts—a tour of the human heart. Discovery Reef, a popular spot at the Columbus Zoo, is a coral reef in a 100,000-gallon (378,540 l) water tank. More than 1,000 animals live in Discovery Reef.

Opposite: The Holden Arboretum in Kirtland

Many young people enjoy the Center of Science and Industry.

German Village is an old-fashioned neighborhood of restaurants, shops, and homes from the 1800s. The smells of German beer-making used to waft through the air in the nearby Brewery District. Now the old breweries have become restaurants, shops—and new breweries.

Barbie-doll collectors, stand back! The largest Barbie doll in the world reigns over the Barbieland Room in the Mid-Ohio Historical Museum. She's just one of the thousands of dolls in this Canal Winchester museum, outside of Columbus. One of Ohio's many presidential sites is in Marion, north of Columbus. There, visitors can tour the restored home of President Warren G. Harding, where he made hundreds of speeches, and visit his tomb.

Capitol Square

In Capitol Square stand the statehouse, the senate building, and many statues and monuments honoring Ohio's history. The elegant statehouse is made of limestone quarried on the banks of the Scioto River. Like many state capitols around the country, it was built in the Greek Revival style. This style of architecture appealed to the newly independent United States because Greece was one of the world's earliest democracies. The statehouse's tall front columns and center rotunda are typical of the Greek style.

The senate building used to be the supreme court building, but now it houses senators' offices. Its Grand Stair Hall is named for its white marble stairway. Overhead, a ceiling painted with murals surrounds a stained-glass seal of Ohio. Around the statehouse are four Civil War–era cannons manufactured in Greenwood, Ohio. Statues of Christopher Columbus, President William McKinley, and other historical figures stand around the spacious square. ■

Johnny Appleseed

John Chapman showed up in Licking Creek in 1801, his packhorse weighed down with burlap bags. When he got to a clearing, he opened a bag and took out some apple seeds. After carefully planting them, he vanished into the forest, only to repeat his strange ritual again and again. Born in Massachusetts in 1774, this plant lover and missionary wandered through Ohio for more than thirty years, planting apple trees and then coming back to prune them. People called him Johnny Appleseed. He often read aloud from the Bible and performed many acts of kindness toward people and animals. Johnny never ate meat and never carried a gun. Instead, he swapped apple seedlings for a meal and a bed. ■

The Southwest

Cincinnati is a city of rolling hills and river views. It began in 1788 as a settlement on the Ohio River. By the mid-1800s, it was an important rail center and the nation's pork-packing capital. Now high-rise office buildings overlook the Ohio River, with hills rising just beyond them. Mount Adams offers a stunning view of the downtown area and the Ohio River. Barges and steamboats pulled in and out of Cincinnati when it was a bustling river port. Visitors can imagine those days as they take riverboat rides on the Ohio.

Britain's Sir Winston Churchill called Cincinnati "the most beautiful of the inland cities of the Union." The downtown area was truly designed with beauty in mind. Small parks and big outdoor sculptures seem to be around every corner. Fountain Square is a favorite place to read, watch people, or rest from shopping around the square. The magnificent Tyler-Davidson Fountain, built in the 1800s, stands in the center.

Ohio cities and interstates

Nearby are the Contemporary Arts Center and the Taft Museum. The Music Hall is the home of Cincinnati's orchestra, opera, and ballet. This historic building looks like a castle, with glittering chandeliers overhead and richly carved woodwork.

West of downtown is the Cincinnati Museum Center. This huge complex occupies Union Terminal, a majestic railway station built in the art deco style. Today, it houses the Cincinnati Historical Society Museum, the Museum of Natural History and Science, and the Children's Discovery Center. The natural history museum has a model of Cincinnati in the Ice Age. The historical society reproduces an 1850s version of Cincinnati's riverfront.

Opposite: The Cincinnati skyline at dusk

Cincinnati from the Kentucky side of the Ohio River

Eden Park, northeast of downtown, is a hilly nature preserve with walking and biking trails. Within the park is the Cincinnati Art Museum, one of the finest in the country. Also in Eden Park are the Playhouse in the Park and Krohn Conservatory, one of the country's largest public greenhouses.

Cincinnati has preserved many of its historic neighborhoods and their original homes. Over-the-Rhine is an old German community with red-brick buildings along its steep roads. Victorian-style homes line the streets in the West End. Presidential sites abound in the Cincinnati area too. Memorials mark the birthplaces of William Howard Taft and Ulysses S. Grant and the tomb of William Henry Harrison.

For Cincinnati residents, going to Kentucky is as easy as going to the suburbs. Kentucky is just across the John A. Roebling Suspension Bridge from the downtown waterfront. Covington Landing, on the Kentucky side of the river, is a huge floating entertainment complex.

Up the Ohio River at Ripley stands Rankin House, where the Rankin family harbored hundreds of escaped slaves. Not far away is Georgetown, Ulysses S. Grant's boyhood home. Near Lebanon, on the way to Dayton, is Fort Ancient, a settlement of the prehistoric Hopewell people.

Dayton, known as the birthplace of aviation, was the home of flight pioneers Orville and Wilbur Wright. That makes it the perfect place for the U.S. Air Force Museum. More than 300 aircraft displayed on its 10 acres (4 ha) of exhibits span the history of flight from balloons to B-1 bombers. Thrilling films in the IMAX theater put visitors right in the cockpit.

At the Dayton Museum of Discovery, young people learn about physics as they climb the soaring Discovery Tower. Back on the ground, native Ohio animals go about their lives in the indoor zoo.

The home of African-American poet Paul Laurence Dunbar contains mementos of his life and career. The Dayton Art Institute covers 5,000 years of art history. Dayton's oldest "neighborhood"—Sun Watch Prehistoric Indian Village—is rebuilt on its original foundations of 800 years ago. Visitors can walk through the Indians' homes and gardens and learn how they used astronomy.

Annie Oakley

Annie Oakley (1860–1926) was a world-famous sharpshooter. She was born in Darke County, in far-western Ohio, and her real name was Phoebe Ann Moses. At age fifteen, she traveled to Cincinnati for a shooting match. She won, beating Frank Butler, the world's best marksman at that time. Later, the two fell in love and were married. They joined Buffalo Bill's Wild West Show, in which Annie was the star shooter. She could hit the thin edge of a playing card and shoot a dime thrown into the air. Annie even performed for Queen Victoria of England. Irving Berlin told her life's story in his musical *Annie Get Your Gun* (1946). In Greenville, a memorial statue and the Garst Museum honor Annie and her amazing skills. ∎

The Northwest

Toledo, the third-largest Great Lakes port, calls itself the glass capital of the world. Both the Toledo Museum of Art and the University Arts Center highlight the history of the city's rich history of glassmaking. The museum displays hundreds of glass objects dating from ancient times until today. Visitors can tour the city's glass factories and shop at its many outlet stores.

The Maumee River flows through Toledo on its way to Lake Erie. Residents stroll along the river walk and relax in riverfront parks. Another place to relax is the botanical garden, with its thousands of flower and tree species and beautiful landscapes.

Both Toledo and Columbus have a COSI—a Center of Science and Industry. At Toledo's center, visitors experience an awesome lightning show and a hair-raising high-wire cycle ride. At the Toledo Zoo, hippopotamuses cavort in their very own Hippoquarium.

Sauder Farm and Craft Village, west of Toledo, brings Ohio's history to life. Costumed villagers demonstrate blacksmithing, quilting, and other pioneer crafts, explaining as they go along. In September, their huge copper kettles simmer with delicious apple butter. The Wolcott House Museum Complex in Maumee preserves a pioneer's log cabin, the Wolcott House, and other buildings from the 1800s. Maumee also honors Ohio baseball heroes in the Ohio Baseball Hall of Fame.

The Toledo Zoo is known for its Hippoquarium.

The North-Central Region

Several islands are clustered along Lake Erie east of Toledo. From South Bass Island, Commodore Oliver Hazard Perry sailed out of Put-in-Bay to fight the Battle of Lake Erie. Perry's Victory and International Peace Memorial commemorates his victory at Put-in-Bay's harbor. The memorial's observation deck offers a view all the way across the lake to Canada. Around the harbor, Victorian-style shops serve vacationers who arrive in their boats.

On Kelleys Island is Inscription Rock, where ancient Indians etched pictures of birds and animals. The island's Glacial Grooves are deep trenches gouged out by glaciers 30,000 years ago.

Cedar Point Amusement Park, on Sandusky's lakefront, has twelve roller coasters—the biggest cluster of "scream machines"

The north shore of Kelleys Island

in the world. The Mantis is the world's tallest, fastest, and steepest stand-up roller coaster. For gentler thrills, there are also Kiddy Kingdom, for younger children, and an old-fashioned carousel.

Malabar Farm in Lucas was the estate of Louis Bromfield, an Ohio author who became a Hollywood screenwriter. In 1945, his friend Humphrey Bogart married Lauren Bacall in the farm's gracious, thirty-two-room mansion. Producer Sam Goldwyn and actor James Cagney were among Bromfield's many famous houseguests. Today, the estate is a state park, offering wagon rides as well as tours of the Big House.

Mansfield has a Hollywood connection, too. Film directors like to shoot prison scenes at Mansfield Reformatory. Four movies, including *Air Force One* and *The Shawshank Redemption*, were filmed there. Visitors can tour the castlelike prison and see the movie sets that were built there. In downtown Mansfield, they can ride a hand-carved wooden carousel and watch craftspeople carving carousel ponies.

The Northeast

Part of northeast Ohio is called colonial country. Its first residents were settlers from the New England colonies, and many buildings feature the colonial architecture style. The region's brightly colored autumn leaves also resemble the fall colors of New England.

The first New Englander to arrive was Moses Cleveland of Connecticut. With a group of explorers, he hacked his way through the wilderness to set up "New Connecticut." In 1796, he built a town at the mouth of the Cuyahoga River. It grew from a population of seven in 1800 to more than half a million today. Legend says that the *a* was dropped from Cleveland's name because a typesetter at the local newspaper couldn't fit it all on one line.

Sitting on Lake Erie at the river's mouth, Cleveland grew into an important shipping center. With iron ore from across the Great Lakes, it also became a major steel producer. Cleveland's wealthy families lived in elegant mansions along Euclid Avenue, called "Millionaire's Row."

Cleveland was named for Moses Cleaveland, who founded the city in 1796.

As in many of the large U.S. cities, Cleveland's downtown area deteriorated over time as more residents moved to the suburbs. But renewal projects have put a new face on the city center. Now a grassy park called Public Square sits right in the center of Cleveland's business district. At one end looms a 52-story skyscraper called Terminal Tower. This former train station was once the tallest U.S. building outside Manhattan. Today, it offers a sweeping view of the city, lakefront, and surrounding suburbs. Downtown shoppers love the five-story Cleveland Arcade, a beautiful piece of architecture built in 1890.

Imagine playing a jukebox with more than 25,000 tunes. Or watching your favorite rock stars in concert on a two-story screen. Or seeing Michael Jackson's jeweled glove and John Lennon's collarless jacket with your own eyes. That's some of what awaits you at the Rock and Roll Hall of Fame.

Opened in 1995, the supermodern "glass pyramid on the lake" was designed by world-famous architect I. M. Pei. Visitors explore the world of rock and roll through interactive exhibits, rockers' instruments and clothes, and videos of memorable moments in rock and roll history.

The Hall of Fame is just one attraction in the North Coast Harbor area, however. Another is the Great Lakes Science Center. It offers more than 350 interactive exhibits for curious and adventuresome visitors. Nearby is the William J. Mather Museum, a real steamship that once hauled iron ore on Lake Erie. On board, visitors explore the history of Cleveland's shipping days.

A dozen museums cluster around University Circle, east of downtown. Lucy—her skeleton, actually—is the most famous resident of the Cleveland Museum of Natural History. She's one of the oldest humans ever discovered. Flowers and fountains surround the Cleveland Museum of Art. Among its many artworks is a fabulous collection of Asian art. The Western Reserve Historical Society preserves artifacts of the Shaker religious group.

Other sites in the circle are the children's museum, the Crawford Auto-Aviation Museum, and the Center for Contemporary Art. The Circle's Severance Hall is home to the world-class Cleveland Orchestra. The landmark building features red marble columns, inlaid wood panels, and silver-leaf ceilings.

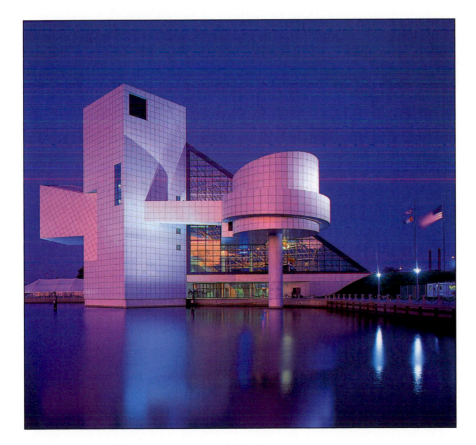

**The Rock and Roll
Hall of Fame**

Cleveland's professional sports teams play right downtown in the Gateway sports complex. It includes a huge basketball arena for the Cleveland Cavaliers and Jacobs Field, home of the Cleveland Indians baseball team.

President James A. Garfield and his wife, Lucretia, rest in Lake View Cemetery. So does millionaire John D. Rockefeller. Their ornate mausoleums are the handiwork of Italian artisans who lived in the nearby Little Italy neighborhood. Tremont, high on a hilltop, is an old Polish neighborhood with onion-domed churches and savory-smelling restaurants.

Thousands of exotic animals live at Cleveland Metroparks Zoo. Tropical species make their home in a rain-forest jungle, complete with a waterfall and a replica of an ancient temple.

Shamu the performing whale is a popular attraction at Sea World, in the suburb of Aurora. Next to Sea World is Geauga Lake

The Day of the Buzzards

March 15 is the Day of the Buzzards in Hinckley, a small town southwest of Cleveland. People gather there from miles around, each hoping to spot the first buzzard of the season. According to legend, in 1818, the townspeople of Hinckley were running out of food. Bears and wolves were destroying their farm animals, and they needed food for the winter. At sunrise on Christmas Eve, about 600 men and boys gath- ered in the forest, and the hunt began. When it was over, they had taken seventeen wolves, twenty-one bears, and three hundred deer, as well as foxes, raccoons, and turkeys. Everyone took what they needed to survive the winter. But when the snows melted, the left-over carcasses sent up a terrible smell. Buzzards swarmed in for the remains, and they have returned every year since then. ■

Amusement Park. Its Mind Eraser roller coaster blows riders' minds with its backward loops.

Cuyahoga Valley National Recreation Area stretches along the Cuyahoga River between Cleveland and Akron. Its scenic railroad chugs through the valley, giving riders an eyeful of changing leaves in the fall. In the winter, people flock to the valley's ski slopes and enjoy horse-drawn sleigh rides.

Kids discover their own inventive nature in Akron's Inventure Place. They can make a percussion band using laser beams or animate their own cartoons. Within the complex is the National Inventors Hall of Fame. It follows the creative process of Thomas Edison, Alexander Graham Bell, and other great inventors.

Stan Hywet Hall in Akron once belonged to industrialist Frank Seiberling.

What was life like for Akron's rubber kings? At least part of the answer lies in Stan Hywet Hall. This sixty-five-room millionaire's mansion sparkles with glowing chandeliers, oriental carpets, and medieval tapestries. The estate belonged to Frank Seiberling, who helped start Goodyear Tire and Rubber Company.

Canton, the birthplace of the National Football League, is the natural spot for the Pro Football Hall of Fame. It fills up five buildings, with exhibits ranging from early football memorabilia to action-packed NFL films. A rotating, multisensory theater takes visitors into the locker room, through the tunnel, and onto the field for a huge-screen Stadium Show.

For a gentler experience, visitors can ride the antique carousel at Canton's Merry-Go-Round Museum. Hundred-year-old horseless buggies and other early cars are on display at Canton's Classic Car Museum.

Amish Country

South of Canton, the countryside spreads out into simple, rustic farms that seem to belong to another age. For the Amish people who live there, time truly has stood still. They have kept a simple, modest way of life since they arrived almost 200 years ago. Horse-drawn buggies clatter along the roads, and sturdy horses pull the plows.

Schoenbrunn, near New Philadelphia, was the site of Ohio's first Christian settlement. David Zeisberger founded it in 1772 as a Moravian mission, but Revolutionary War battles forced the people to abandon their town in 1776. Today, its rebuilt log buildings give visitors a glimpse of missionary life in the frontier wilderness.

Amish in Walnut Creek

The Amish arrived from Switzerland and Germany, and many other Swiss and German people settled in this area too. The countryside reminded them of the land they left behind. Sugarcreek, called Little Switzerland, looks like a charming Swiss village. Storefronts are painted with mountain scenery, and polka music drifts through the air. Visitors can watch the old Swiss art of cheesemaking at Broadrum Cheesehouse. From Sugarcreek, the Ohio Central Railroad offers a steam-train tour of Amish country.

Berlin is a center for both the Amish and their religious kinspeople, the Mennonites. At the Mennonite Information Center, a cyclorama, or circular painting, surrounds the viewer for 265 feet (81 m). This dramatic mural depicts the history of Amish and Mennonite people from their beginnings in Switzerland in 1525.

The Sherman Brothers

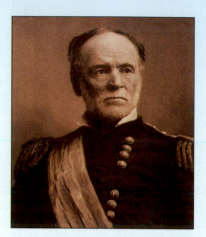

Lancaster was the birthplace of two famous brothers—Civil War general William Tecumseh Sherman (above) and Senator John Sherman (right). General Sherman (1820–1891) led the Union campaign through Georgia and the Carolinas, known as Sherman's March to the Sea. "War is hell," he once said, "and you cannot refine it." When asked to run for president in 1884, Sherman gave the famous reply: "If nominated, I will not accept; if elected, I will not serve."

John Sherman (1823–1900) had a long political career. He served as a U.S. senator from Ohio (1861–1877 and 1881–1897), secretary of the treasury (1877–1881), and secretary of state (1897–1898). His greatest achievement was the Sherman Antitrust Act, which he pushed through Congress. It still stands as a watchdog on powerful companies.

Both Shermans were born in Lancaster's Sherman House, now a national historic landmark. They became orphans in 1829, when William was nine and John was six. ■

The Southeast

Chillicothe, the capital of the Northwest Territory, became the first state capital in 1803. Its name comes from a Shawnee word meaning "town." Today Chillicothe is a manufacturing center, but much remains from the old days.

Thomas Worthington, one of Ohio's founders, lived in an eighteen-room mansion overlooking the Scioto River. Now it's a landmark on the luxuriant grounds of Adena State Memorial. Two thousand years earlier, in nearby Mound City, Hopewell people

**Hocking Hills
State Park**

built huge mounds surrounded by an earthen wall. Beautiful arti-facts have been found inside the mounds.

Hocking Hills State Park is a breathtaking expanse of water-falls, deep gorges, caves, and strange sandstone rock formations. Foxes dart among the wildflowers and ferns in the cool shade of towering hemlocks. Hikers meander through deep valleys along the Buckeye Trail or enjoy the view from the top of the Rim Trail. Old Man's Cave was the home of Civil War fugitive Richard Rowe for years. Indians once camped at Ash Cave, alongside a 90-foot

Wayne National Forest is just one of Ohio's many parks.

The Coonskin Library

Imagine strolling into your public library, finding the books you want, then swaggering up to the desk and slapping down a raccoon skin! That's just what patrons of the Coonskin Library did. Opened in Amesville in 1803, the Coonskin Library gave pioneers a rare chance to read great works of literature. Some of their favorites were plays by William Shakespeare and tales by Washington Irving. ▪

(27-m) waterfall. Trickling water carved out the rooms of the age-old Rock House, high on the side of a cliff.

From Nelsonville, the Hocking Valley Scenic Railway chugs into the hills and valleys of Wayne National Forest. It makes a stop at Robbins' Crossing, where a museum recreates country life in the 1850s. Visitors can drive winding roads through the forest and cross the covered bridges that horse-drawn carriages used to take.

The Muskingum River Parkway cruises along the river and its historic locks. In the 1840s, the hand-operated locks controlled heavy traffic—hundreds of paddle-wheeled steamboats. And traffic is still heavy today, with motorboats and houseboats honking their horns as they approach the locks. At the McConnelsville

Lock, visitors can watch the scene while they picnic along the riverbanks.

Marietta was the first settlement in Ohio and the first in the Northwest Territory. Sitting at the juncture of the Muskingum and Ohio Rivers, it became an important steamboat port. Today, visitors can see an old-time steamboat at the Ohio River Museum. As they take a steamboat ride up the river, they can imagine those days when steam power ushered in an exciting new age for Ohio—and for the whole nation.

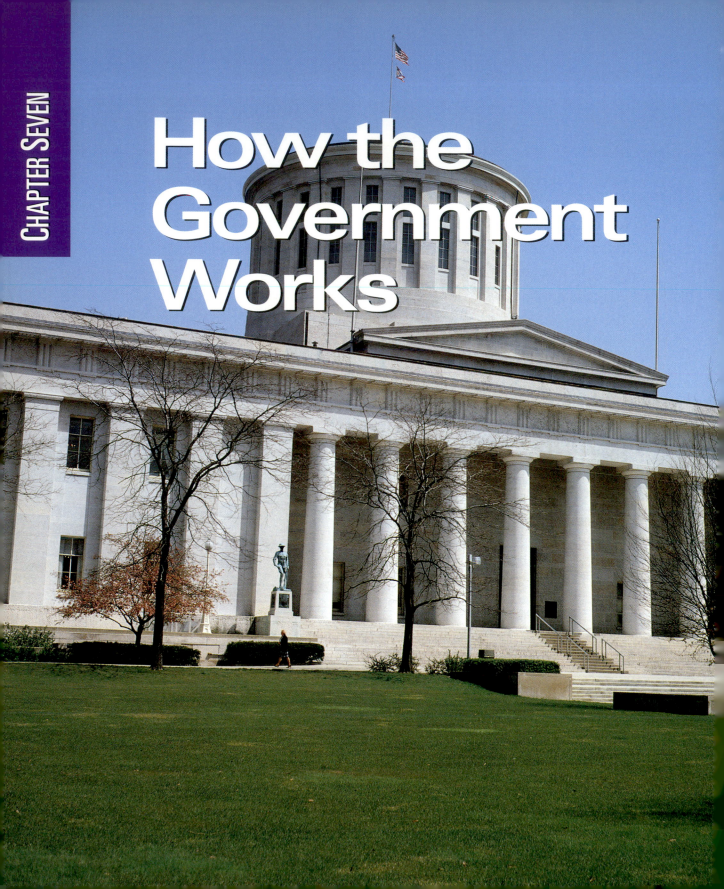

CHAPTER SEVEN

How the Government Works

When Edward Tiffin took office as Ohio's first governor, there wasn't much he could do. And the next twenty governors couldn't do much either. By the rules of the 1802 constitution, the legislature got to appoint all state officers except the governor. In 1850, a constitutional convention met to draw up a new constitution. The constitution of 1851, giving the governor much broader powers, is still in effect today.

Inside the state senate chamber

Sometimes Ohioans want to amend, or change, their constitution. They may change an old provision in the constitution or add something new. If 10 percent of the voters sign a petition for the amendment, it goes to the legislature for approval. After passing both houses of the legislature, it goes back to the people for a final vote. Members of the legislature may also propose an amendment. Both legislators and voters must approve it.

Every twenty years, voters have a chance to call for a constitutional convention. Such a convention could pass new amendments—or write a whole new constitution.

Ohio's government is organized like the U.S. government. Power is balanced among the executive, legislative, and judicial branches. The three branches keep a check on one another so that no one branch becomes too powerful or too weak.

Opposite: The Ohio state capitol

Ohio's State Symbols

State animal: White-tailed deer White-tailed deer used to be rare in Ohio. Today, they are found in every county, but about 80 percent of them live in the eastern Ohio hills.

State bird: Cardinal Cardinals (left) live in the state of Ohio all year round. Their song is a strong, clear "Cheer! Cheer!" Male cardinals are a brilliant red, while females are brown with reddish wings. Cardinals have stout beaks that are good for cracking seeds and nuts.

State flower: Scarlet carnation Ohio adopted its state flower in memory of a beloved native son—President William McKinley. McKinley very rarely appeared in public without a red carnation in his lapel. His assassination in 1901 was a grave loss to America, and especially to Ohioans who knew and loved him.

State tree: Ohio buckeye The large, brown seeds of the buckeye tree look like the brown eyes of a male white-tailed deer, or buck. Native Americans were the first to use the name. Now buckeye is the nickname for both Ohio and its inhabitants. Buckeye trees usually grow to about 40 feet (12 m). But Ohio's tallest buckeye, in Hamilton County, stands 82 feet (25 m) high.

State wildflower: White trillium The white trillium (below left) is a member of the lily family. Its leaves grow in groups of three, and its three-petaled white flower perches atop an erect stem. The white trillium grows in every Ohio county. Its scientific name is *Trillium grandiflorum*.

State reptile: Black racer snake When Jacob Mercer was in the fourth grade, he wrote a letter to his state legislators. Jacob suggested that the lawmakers name an official state reptile. He and his classmates picked the black racer snake because it lives in all eighty-eight Ohio counties. It's also known as the "farmer's friend" because it eats rodents that carry diseases. The legislature was convinced! In 1995, it passed a resolution naming the black racer snake as the official state reptile.

State fossil: Trilobite Ohio's state fossil, the isotelus, is commonly known as the trilobite. This now-extinct invertebrate (spineless) arthropod is named for its three-lobed body. Trilobites lived in Ohio during the Ordovician period—about 440 million years ago—when saltwater seas covered the state. Most trilobites were under 4 inches (10 cm) long. Scientists discovered the largest known complete trilobite fossil at Huffman Dam in Montgomery County.

State insect: Ladybug Ladybugs, or ladybird beetles (right), are beautifully colored orange insects with black spots. According to state legislators, Ohioans love ladybugs for many reasons. They say the "queenly" ladybug is both proud and friendly, as Ohioans are. The bug is also industrious and hardy, keeping its beauty and charm under tough living conditions. Finally, the ladybug is in tune with Ohio's commitment to conservation because it consumes millions of harmful insects.

State gemstone: Ohio Flint Flint is a smooth, hard type of quartz. It was formed from tightly compressed sediment that once sank to the seafloor. Ohio's Native Americans chipped flint to make knives, spear points, and arrowheads. Later, settlers used flint to make the explosive spark in their flintlock guns. They also used enormous flint stones as millstones for grinding grain.

State beverage: Tomato juice Ohio leads the United States in the production of tomato juice and is second only to California in overall tomato production.

State rock song: "Hang on Sloopy" Written by Rick Derringer from Celina, this song was adopted in 1985.

Ohio's State Song

"Beautiful Ohio"
Music by Mary Earl, words by Ballard MacDonald

I sailed away;
Wandered afar;
Crossed the mighty restless sea;
Looked for where I ought to be.
Cities so grand, mountains above,
Led to this land I love.

Chorus:
Beautiful Ohio, where the golden grain
Dwarf the lovely flowers in the summer rain.
Cities rising high, silhouette the sky.

Freedom is supreme in this majestic land;
Mighty factories seem to hum in tune, so grand.
Beautiful Ohio, thy wonders are in view,
Land where my dreams all come true!

The State Flag and Seal

Adopted in 1902, Ohio's state flag is pennant shaped with a swallowtail point. The flag has a blue triangle on the left, representing Ohio's hills and valleys, with red and white stripes to symbolize roads and waterways. On the triangle are seventeen stars and a large white O

with a red center. Thirteen of the stars are for the original colonies, with four more to show that Ohio was the seventeenth state. The *O* in the triangle stands for Ohio and also resembles a buckeye, hearkening back to the state's nickname.

Ohio's state seal was chosen in 1967 with changes made in 1996. In the background, a sun with thirteen rays—for the thirteen colonies—comes up over Mount Logan, showing that this was the first state west of the Allegheny Mountains and the

first state in the Northwest Territory. Flowing in front of Mount Logan is the Scioto River, with fields in the foreground. Also in front are a bundle of wheat—representing the state's agriculture—and seventeen arrows as a reminder that Ohio was the seventeenth state. ■

The Executive Branch

Governor Robert and Hope Taft

The executive branch makes sure Ohio's laws are carried out. Ohio's governor is the state's chief executive and the head of the executive branch. Voters elect the governor to a four-year term. In Ohio, a governor may serve any number of terms but only two terms in a row. After two terms as governor, a person has to wait four years before running again.

The governor appoints cabinet members, or advisors, to direct many of the state's agencies and departments. These include the departments of agriculture, budget and management, commerce, education, environmental protection, health, and transportation. The state board of education is part of the executive branch, too. The governor appoints the trustees of state universities.

Other executive officers are the lieutenant governor, secretary

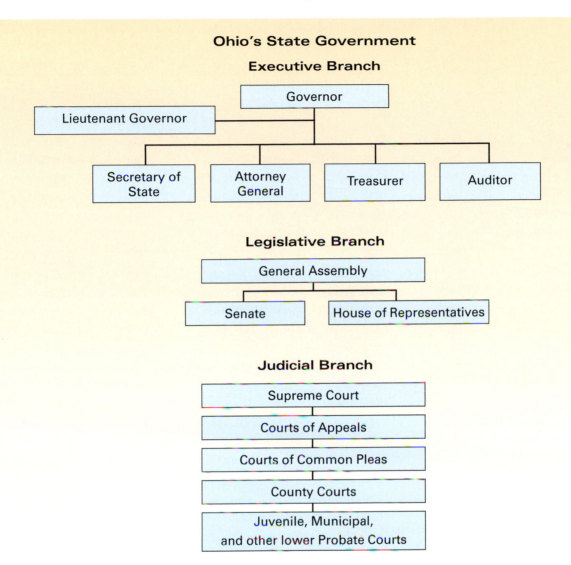

Ohio's State Government

Executive Branch

- Governor
- Lieutenant Governor
- Secretary of State
- Attorney General
- Treasurer
- Auditor

Legislative Branch

- General Assembly
  - Senate
  - House of Representatives

Judicial Branch

- Supreme Court
- Courts of Appeals
- Courts of Common Pleas
- County Courts
- Juvenile, Municipal, and other lower Probate Courts

of state, attorney general, treasurer, and auditor. Voters elect them all to four-year terms. Like the governor, they may not serve more than two terms in a row.

Each of these officers has a big job to do. The lieutenant governor is second in command. Whenever the governor cannot carry

Ohio's Governors

Name	Party	Term	Name	Party	Term
Edward Tiffin	Dem.-Rep.	1803–1807	Richard M. Bishop	Dem	1878–1880
Thomas Kirker	Dem.-Rep.	1807–1808	Charles Foster	Rep.	1880–1884
Samuel Huntington	Dem.-Rep.	1808–1810	George Hoadly	Dem.	1884–1886
Return J. Meigs Jr.	Dem.-Rep.	1810–1814	Joseph B. Foraker	Rep.	1886–1890
Othneil Looker	Dem.-Rep	1814	James E. Campbell	Dem.	1890–1892
Thomas Worthington	Dem.-Rep.	1814–1818	William McKinley	Rep.	1892–1896
Ethan Allen Brown	Dem.-Rep.	1818–1822	Asa S. Bushnell	Rep.	1896–1900
Allen Trimble	Fed.	1822	George K. Nash	Rep.	1900–1904
Jeremiah Morrow	Dem.-Rep.	1822–1826	Myron T. Herrick	Rep.	1904–1906
Allen Trimble	Fed.	1826–1830	John M. Pattison	Dem.	1906
Duncan McArthur	Fed.	1830–1832	Andrew L. Harris	Rep.	1906–1909
Robert Lucas	Dem.	1832–1836	Judson Harmon	Dem.	1909–1913
Joseph Vance	Whig	1836–1838	James M. Cox	Dem.	1913–1915
Wilson Shannon	Dem.	1838–1840	Frank B. Willis	Rep.	1915–1917
Thomas Corwin	Whig	1840–1842	James M. Cox	Dem.	1917–1921
Wilson Shannon	Dem.	1842–1844	Harry L. Davis	Rep.	1921–1923
Thomas W. Bartley	Dem.	1844	A. Victor Donahey	Dem.	1923–1929
Mordecai Bartley	Whig	1844–1846	Myers Y. Cooper	Rep.	1929–1931
William Bebb	Whig	1846–1849	George White	Dem.	1931–1935
Seabury Ford	Whig	1849–1850	Martin L. Davey	Dem.	1935–1939
Reuben Wood	Dem.	1850–1853	John W. Bricker	Rep.	1939–1945
William Medill	Dem.	1853–1856	Frank J. Lausche	Dem.	1945–1947
Salmon P. Chase	Rep.	1856–1860	Thomas J. Herbert	Rep.	1947–1949
William Dennison Jr.	Rep.	1860–1862	Frank J. Lausche	Dem.	1949–1957
David Todd	Rep.	1862–1864	John W. Brown	Rep.	1957
John Brough	Rep.	1864–1865	C. William O'Neill	Rep.	1957–1959
Charles Anderson	Rep.	1865–1866	Michael V. DiSalle	Dem.	1959–1963
Jacob Dolson Cox	Rep.	1866–1868	James A. Rhodes	Rep.	1963–1971
Rutherford B. Hayes	Rep.	1868–1872	John J. Gilligan	Dem.	1971–1975
Edward F. Noyes	Rep.	1872–1874	James A. Rhodes	Rep.	1975–1983
William Allen	Dem.	1874–1876	Richard F. Celeste	Dem.	1983–1991
Rutherford B. Hayes	Rep.	1876–1877	George V. Voinovich	Rep.	1991–1999
Thomas L. Young	Rep.	1877–1878	Robert Taft	Rep.	1999–

out all of his or her duties, the lieutenant governor steps in. The secretary of state oversees elections and grants companies permission to do business in Ohio. The attorney general is the state's top lawyer and law-enforcement officer. Collecting, investing, and protecting the state's money is the treasurer's job. In simple terms, the auditor balances the state's checkbook and writes all its checks.

The Legislature

Ohio's legislature, or lawmaking body, is called the general assembly. Like the U.S. Congress, it is bicameral, or made up of two houses—the senate and the house of representatives. Voters elect thirty-three senators and ninety-nine representatives to the general assembly. Senators can serve a maximum of two four-year terms in a row. Representatives are elected to two-year terms and can serve up to four consecutive terms.

The Legislative Service Commission works closely with the general assembly. This group of legal experts takes a proposed law and writes an explanation of it in clear language. The commission also makes sure the laws are worded in proper legal form.

In 1903, Ohioans passed an amendment that gave each county at least one representative, no matter how small the county was. It seemed like a good idea at the time. However, in 1964, the U.S. Supreme Court ruled that this plan violated the U.S. Constitution because it didn't give all Ohioans an equal voice in their government.

State officials then sat down with a map and population tables to reapportion, or redraw, the legislative districts. The result was a

Taft Family Politics

For the Tafts, politics is a family business. President William Howard Taft's father, Alphonso Taft (above), was U.S. secretary of war, attorney general, and minister to Austria-Hungary and Russia. The president's son and grandson became U.S. senators. Robert Taft, the president's great-grandson, served in the Ohio House of Representatives (1976–1980) and was Ohio's secretary of state (1991–1999). In 1998, he was elected governor of Ohio. ■

Governor George Voinovich, in that office from 1991 to 1999, delivering a State of the State address in 1998.

plan that divided the state into thirty-three senatorial districts and ninety-nine representative districts. Districts within each category have roughly the same number of people.

Now Ohio redraws its districts every ten years. This ensures that all citizens are fairly represented as the population grows and population centers shift.

The Courts

Ohio's court system makes up the judicial branch of state government. Judges on the courts are experts on state laws. They decide whether someone has broken the law.

The Ohio Supreme Court is the state's highest court. Its chief justice and six associate justices are elected to six-year terms. The supreme court is Ohio's court of last resort. Defendants who disagree with the outcome of a case may appeal the decision to a higher court. But once the supreme court makes a ruling, all appeals are over.

The supreme court can also inquire about unlawful imprisonment, order public officials to perform their duties, or order a lower court to stop abusing its powers. Another duty of the supreme

The Astronaut Senator

John H. Glenn Jr. was born in Cambridge in 1921 and attended Muskingum College. In 1962, aboard the Mercury capsule *Friendship 7*, he became the first U.S. astronaut to orbit Earth. After retiring from his astronaut career, Glenn was elected to the U.S. Senate in 1974. In 1998, at the age of seventy-seven, Glenn took to the skies again. He became the oldest person in space when he joined the crew of the space shuttle *Discovery*. ■

court is to review every case in which the defendant has been sentenced to death.

Beneath the supreme court are twelve district courts of appeals. Each district has three to twelve judges who are elected to six-year terms. Their main job is to hear cases appealed from lower courts. Each county has a court of common pleas. These courts handle civil and criminal cases, family law, and juvenile offenses. There are also regular county courts and municipal courts. The court of claims hears lawsuits against the state of Ohio.

How Ohio's Laws Are Made

Every state law begins as an idea. Once a senator or representative introduces the idea in the general assembly, it's called a bill. First the bill goes to the appropriate committee. For example, if the bill is about school lunches, it would go to the education committee. Members in the "house of origin" then debate the bill and often change parts of it in the process.

Finally, when all discussions are over, the members take a vote. If more than half of them approve the bill, it goes on to the assembly's other house. There the process begins all over again.

Once both houses have passed the bill, it goes to the governor. The governor has ten days to either sign the bill or veto it. If the governor signs the bill, it becomes a law. If the governor vetoes it, the bill goes back to the general assembly.

At this point, it takes a three-fifths vote in both houses of the assembly to override the veto and make the bill a law. If the governor does nothing in the ten-day period, the bill automatically becomes a law.

Ohio's counties

Local Government

Ohio is divided into eighty-eight counties. By law, each county has the right to home rule—that is, to organize its government in any way it chooses. So far, only Summit County has taken this option. Its voters elect a county executive and a seventeen-member county council. All the other counties elect a three-member board of commissioners.

There are no towns in Ohio! There are only cities and villages. Officially, a city is a community of 5,000 or more people. Communities with fewer than 5,000 people are called villages. Cities and villages can choose home rule, too, and about one-fourth of them have done so. They may be governed by a city commission or by a city council with a mayor or city manager.

A Swingin' State

When national elections roll around, Ohio is known as a swing state. That is, it might swing either way—Democratic or Republican. But Ohio is more than just a big question mark. Smart politicians pay close attention to the way Ohioans vote. Why? Because whichever way Ohio swings, the whole country is likely to swing that way, too. Throughout history, Ohio's choice for president has turned out to be the winner an overwhelming number of times. As Ohioans see it, that's only natural. After all, they produced eight presidents—so they certainly know how to pick one!

Some Ohio villages, such as Chagrin Falls, have chosen home rule and are governed by a city commission or city council.

CHAPTER EIGHT

Ohioans at Work

I n 1870, Benjamin F. Goodrich rounded up a handful of Akron businessmen. They invested $1,000 each in Goodrich's new venture—a factory that made fire hoses. Ten years later, when business was slow, the investors all pulled out. Mistake!

In the 1890s, Americans were taking their first joy rides in "horseless carriages." The drive was smoother than a buggy ride because Goodrich provided the wheels. He'd invented the pneumatic tire—an air-filled tube, sort of like a rubber hose molded into a circle. Firestone, Goodyear, and other companies soon joined Akron's rubber-tire boom. That's how Akron got to be called the Rubber Capital of the World.

Another man of vision launched the state's steel industry. When iron ore was discovered in the Mahoning Valley, Daniel Heaton had an idea. In 1804, he built an iron-smelting furnace near Youngstown, using charcoal to keep the fires blazing. Heaton

Ohio's steel industry is important for the state's economy.

Opposite: Outside a limestone plant

poured the sputtering hot liquid into molds to make kettles, skillets, irons, and even stoves. Others followed Heaton's scheme, refining the iron into steel.

Today, only Indiana makes more steel than Ohio does. Ohio ranks third in the nation in the value of its manufactured goods, and the top items are made of steel. Ohio is the nation's number-one manufacturer of automotive parts. Many plants that make car and truck parts are in the southern part of the state.

Ohio is also the second-largest producer of motor vehicles among the states, after Michigan. About one-fourth of all the trucks in the country come from Ohio. Industrial machinery, electrical equipment, household appliances, jet engines, and other aircraft parts roll off Ohio's assembly lines too. It takes highly skilled workers to produce these goods, and Ohio is known for its top-notch industrial engineers. Overall, the state's unemployment rate is low compared to the rest of the nation.

Ohio's chemicals factories make products such as paint, varnish, and soap. Procter & Gamble, the nation's largest soap company, is headquartered in Cincinnati. Food-processing plants turn farm products into cookies, cooking oil, packaged meat and milk, cheese, and beer. Toledo is known for its glassworks, and Ohio River towns make pottery and other items out of clay.

Transport companies also do big business in Ohio. They take factory-made goods and ship them to customers by truck, rail, water, or air. Many of the customers live in other countries. Ohio is the nation's third-largest exporter.

Don't get the idea that factories make everything in Ohio. Craftspeople around Zanesville make handmade pottery and

Ransom Olds

Oldsmobiles were named after Ransom Olds (1864–1950). Born in Geneva, Ohio, Olds became a partner in his father's machine shop in Lansing, Michigan. There he invented an internal combustion engine for automobiles. In 1899, he opened Olds Motor Works in Detroit, where he introduced the Oldsmobile—the first mass-produced car. In 1915, Olds began to produce another of his inventions, the power lawn mower. ■

stoneware. Amish artisans make handsewn quilts, handwoven rugs, and handcrafted furniture. In many products, human skill is more important than the equipment used. That goes for Ohio's candy, cheese, bologna, pasta, wicker baskets, and glass.

Mining

If the entire country had to rely on Ohio for its salt, there would be enough to last—well—forever! Geologists estimate that northeast Ohio's rock-salt beds could supply America for several thousand years. Salt was Ohio's top mineral in the pioneer days. Today, Ohio is the third-largest salt-producing state. The deepest salt

The Vacuum Cleaner Man

People who like to tidy up their homes owe a lot to William Henry Hoover (1849–1932). He made the vacuum cleaner a common household appliance. Born in Stark County, Hoover began a hide-tanning business on the family farm in New Berlin (now North Canton). His business became a real success when he switched to the production of leather goods. In 1908, he bought the patent on an electric cleaning machine from James Murray Spangler. His new business was incorporated as the Electric Suction Sweeper Company. Hoover's vacuum cleaners soon swept the world. ■

Salt is one of the minerals mined in Ohio.

mine in the country sinks down about 2,000 feet (610 m) near Fairport Harbor.

Ohio's mines produce tons of minerals used in construction. The state ranks second in the production of lime, used to make fertilizer; fourth in sand, gravel, and clay; and seventh in crushed stone. Many of these minerals go straight to construction sites for new buildings and highways.

About one-third of the nation's sandstone comes from Ohio. The state's clay is made into bricks, pottery, and ceramic tiles for floors and walls. Limestone is used not only for construction and lime, but also for making glass. A good portion goes to Toledo, which calls itself the glass capital of the world.

Coal is Ohio's most valuable mineral. Most of Ohio's electricity is generated from coal-burning power plants. East and southeast Ohio are part of the Appalachian coalfields that extend into Pennsylvania and West Virginia.

In the 1800s, Ohio's steel mills switched from burning charcoal in their furnaces to burning coal. Coal has been the primary fuel for heavy industries ever since. Now Ohio's power plants use coal, too. Miners used to descend deep into the earth and mine coal in underground shafts. Today, they take coal from strip mines on the surface. Mining companies are required by law to restore the environment after removing the coal.

What Ohio Grows, Manufactures, and Mines

Agriculture	Manufacturing	Mining
Soybeans	Transportation equipment	Coal
Corn	Machinery	Natural gas
Milk	Fabricated metal products	Petroleum
Greenhouse and nursery products	Primary metals	Salt
Hops	Food products	
Beef cattle	Chemicals	

In the 1970s, Ohioans became concerned about air and water pollution from the state's factories. They were especially worried about sulfur dioxide, which is released from burning coal. Since then, engineers have found ways to reduce sulfur emissions in coal-burning plants. Researchers are still working on the problem, since the sulfur-removing process produces harmful by-products, too.

Natural gas and petroleum, or oil, rank second and third among mineral resources in their value to the state. Gas comes mainly from southeastern Ohio, while oil is found in the east and northwest. Ohio has more than 64,000 active oil and gas wells. In the mid-1990s, they produced more than 8.75 million barrels of oil and nearly 130 billion cubic feet of natural gas.

Until the mid-1800s, Ohio's steel mills used iron ore from the state's own mines. However, after a canal was built connecting Lakes Superior and Huron, it became easier and cheaper to import iron ore from Minnesota and other Great Lakes states. Today, Ohio is the nation's second-leading manufacturer of steel, and it still buys its iron ore from outside the state. Ohio also ranks fourth in aluminum, another product made from outside raw materials.

Feeding the World

Just about everyone in Ohio was a farmer in the pioneer days. Cultivating the soil and hunting in the woods were the only ways to get food. By 1850, Ohio was the nation's top agricultural state. Steamboats loaded with Ohio's wheat and pork chugged down the Ohio River and up through the Great Lakes.

Farmland covers more than half of Ohio's land area today. That includes both cropland and pastures for grazing cattle. As in other

Farms in Ohio are getting larger, but the number of farms is growing smaller.

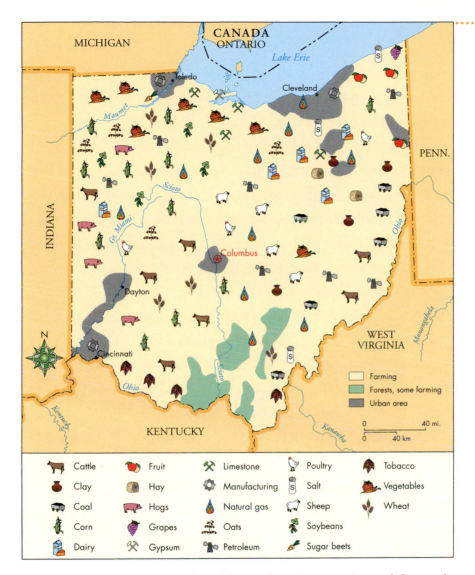

Ohio's natural resources

Map legend:

Farming	Forests, some farming	Urban area	

Cattle	Fruit	Limestone	Poultry	Tobacco
Clay	Hay	Manufacturing	Salt	Vegetables
Coal	Hogs	Natural gas	Sheep	Wheat
Corn	Grapes	Oats	Soybeans	
Dairy	Gypsum	Petroleum	Sugar beets	

states, the farms are getting bigger but the number of farms is shrinking. In 1940, there were about 240,000 farms in Ohio. In 1997, there were only about 73,000.

Ohio's farms yield more than $5.5 billion worth of products. Besides shipping food to other states, Ohio exports tons of farm products to foreign countries. Soybeans are the state's top crop. They account for 22 percent of Ohio's total farm income. Next in importance are corn, milk, chickens and eggs, and greenhouse and nursery products. Ohio farmers also raise hogs, cattle and calves, wheat, oats, and hay, as well as vegetables and fruit.

For farmers who sell fresh vegetables, sweet corn brings in about one-third of their income. Other fresh vegetables from Ohio farms sound like a delicious salad—tomatoes, lettuce, cabbage, celery, cucumbers, onions, and bell peppers. Tomatoes are also processed to make canned tomatoes, tomato juice, and tomato sauce. Apples, peaches, cantaloupes, strawberries, and grapes grow in Ohio, too.

Mercer County leads the other counties in producing hogs and chickens, Wayne County supplies the most milk, and Wood County is first in wheat and soybeans. Ohio ranks fifth in the nation in greenhouse and nursery products, such as cut flowers, potted plants, garden plants, and hanging baskets.

Of all the trees in Ohio, pine is the most valuable for the lumber industry. The thickest pine forests grow in southeastern Ohio. Ash, walnut, oak, cherry, maple, poplar, basswood, and hickory are other important commercial woods.

Ohio Is a Mover!

When a company is looking for a place to build a new factory, Ohio looks great. More new factories open in Ohio every year than in any other state. For one thing, Ohio is within easy reach of consumers. Half the country's population lives within 500 miles (805 km) of its borders. But more important, Ohio is a "mover." It's easy to move goods in and out of the state.

From Lake Erie, ships and barges can easily reach other ports on the Great Lakes. More goods are shipped in and out of Toledo than any other Great Lakes port. Sailing east through the St. Lawrence Seaway, oceangoing vessels can head south to South America or cross the Atlantic to Europe. There is no ship traffic there in the winter, though, because the seaway is frozen, but traffic on the Ohio River goes on all year. More freight moves up and down the Ohio than travels through the Panama Canal.

Ohio's railroads are efficient movers too. Automobile parts, processed foods, tires, and many other goods rely heavily on the rails. Most freight travels on one of Ohio's four large railroad lines. But even short lines such as the Indiana & Ohio Railroad are valuable to manufacturers. And human travelers can reach about ten Ohio cities by train.

In 1797, Ebenezer Zane built a road called Zane's Trace across south-central Ohio from West Virginia to Kentucky. The National Road, or Cumberland Road, was completed through Ohio in 1838. Today, interstate highways make it easy to get almost anywhere in Ohio. Ohio ranks fourth in the nation in interstate mileage and tenth

Freight trains transport food and manufactured goods.

Ohio Astronauts

Along with famous astronaut John Glenn, Neil Armstrong (left) and Judith Resnik were also astronauts who hailed from Ohio. In 1969, Armstrong, born in Wapakoneta, became the first human being to set foot on the moon. Resnik, born in Akron, was the second U.S. woman in space. Tragically, she was killed when the space shuttle *Challenger* exploded shortly after liftoff in 1986. Ohio's other astronauts are James Lovell, Nancy Currie, G. David Low, Robert Overmyer, and Terence Henricks. ■

in total highway miles. The Ohio Turnpike runs across northern Ohio to join the Indiana Toll Road on the west and the Pennsylvania Turnpike on the east.

Thanks to the Wright brothers, Dayton was the site of many exciting breakthroughs in aviation. Ohio is still an important testing ground for experimental aircraft. Ordinary travelers can use more than 180 public airports. The busiest is Cleveland Hopkins International Airport. For people flying in and out of Cincinnati, the most convenient airport is in Boone County, Kentucky.

Getting the Word Out

Only a few hundred people lived in Cincinnati when William Maxwell printed his newspaper there. In the four-page *Centinel of the North-Western Territory*, he reported three-month-old news from Europe and two-week-old news from the Atlantic Coast. But at least he got out the news. The *Centinel*, Ohio's first newspaper, came out in 1793—ten years before Ohio became a state. It was also the first newspaper to be published north and west of the Ohio River.

Maxwell himself was the paper's only reporter, writer, editor, typesetter, and printer. One grouchy reader complained that it told nothing but "meager details of foreign news, no local news, no opinions on county, state or national questions, no lessons from history, no poetry, no wit, no sentiment." Issues of the *Centinel* got farther and farther apart until it folded after three years.

Ohio's newspapers do a much better job today. Many of them are respected and quoted nationwide. The major daily newspapers are the *Cincinnati Enquirer*, the Cleveland *Plain Dealer*, the *Columbus Dispatch*, and the Toledo *Blade*. All of these have been around since the 1800s. About 100 other daily papers and 260 weekly papers are published around the state.

Joseph Medill, founder of the Cleveland *Leader*, was also publisher of the *Chicago Tribune*.

Joseph Medill (1823–1899), who founded the Cleveland *Leader*, later became publisher of the *Chicago Tribune* and mayor of Chicago (1872–1874). Northwestern University's Medill School of Journalism is named in his honor.

Ohio's broadcasting days began in 1922 with Cleveland's WHK radio station. That same year, Ohio State University went on the air with the nation's first educational radio station, WOSU. More than 300 radio stations operate in Ohio today. Television arrived in 1947 with Cleveland's WEWS-TV. Now Ohioans can tune in to about fifty local TV stations.

CHAPTER NINE

People Who Make Ohio Great

O hio was the third-largest state for eighty years— from 1820 to 1900. Only New York and Pennsylvania had larger populations. Then it slipped to fourth place. The 1950 census showed Ohio in fifth place, and in 1970 it dropped to sixth.

Today, Ohio's population is the seventh-largest in the country. According to the 1990 census, more than 10.8 million people live in Ohio. Estimates for 1997 show a population of 11.2 million. That's higher than the populations of Austria, Belgium, Greece, Sweden, or Switzerland.

Ohio may have inched down in rank, but its population has grown steadily since the days of the Northwest Territory. Almost twice as many people live in Ohio today as lived there in 1920.

Since 1970, though, Ohio's population has been growing very slowly. Families are having fewer children, and many people have left the state. Between 1970 to 1990, more people moved out of Ohio than moved in. By the year 2025, the population is expected to grow to only 11.7 million people—just half a million more than in 1997.

Many Ohioans have moved from the cities to the suburbs.

Opposite: All sorts of people live in Ohio.

Population of Ohio's Major Cities (1990)	
Columbus	632,910
Cleveland	505,616
Cincinnati	364,040
Toledo	332,943
Akron	223,019
Dayton	182,044

Cities

About three-fourths of Ohioans live in urban areas—in or near cities. But most big U.S. cities are following a common trend. The city centers are losing residents as more and more people move to suburbs and smaller towns.

Columbus, the state capital, is the largest city in Ohio. About 633,000 people live there. Columbus is the only city in Ohio whose population has not dropped since 1970. Next in order of size are Cleveland and Cincinnati. About two-fifths of Ohio's people live in the metropolitan areas of the top three cities. Toledo, Akron, and Dayton are the next-largest cities.

Where Do Ohioans Come From?

About 88 percent of Ohioans have European ancestors. Many are descendants of the English and Scotch-Irish pioneers who first settled the territory. Later waves of immigration brought people from all over Europe. Most sailed across the Atlantic Ocean into New York City. From there, they made their way west to Ohio's fields and factories.

Some were fleeing religious persecution. People of the Amish, Mennonite, and Hutterite faiths arrived from Germany and Switzerland in the late 1700s and early 1800s. Jewish people began arriving in the late 1880s. They were fleeing bloody massacres in Germany, Poland, and other Eastern European countries. Today, more than 3 million Ohioans claim German ancestry. That's almost 30 percent of the population.

Other immigrants to Ohio faced war, famine, or economic disaster in their homelands. They simply hoped to make a living. In

CANADA
ONTARIO

MICHIGAN

Lake Erie

Toledo

Cleveland

PENN.

INDIANA

Columbus

WEST VIRGINIA

Cincinnati

N

Inhabitants per sq. mi.	Inhabitants per sq km
27–110	10–42
111–204	43–78
205–372	79–143
373–933	144–360
934–1,771	361–683
1,772–3,077	684–1,188

Source: 1990 Census

KENTUCKY

0   40 mi.

0   40 km

Ohio's population density

the early 1800s, miners from Wales came to work the coal mines of southern Ohio. At the same time, a wave of Irish people began to arrive. Their numbers grew in the 1840s during Ireland's potato famine. Many of them helped build Ohio's canals and railroads. By the 1850s, Irish immigrants made up the second-largest ethnic group in Ohio's major cities, after Germans.

Italian immigrants of the late 1800s left behind a country in economic collapse. Along with Poles, Hungarians, Czechs, and Russians, they settled in industrial cities such as Cleveland, Youngstown, and Toledo. Immigrants from Greece, Portugal, China, Japan, Turkey, and dozens of other countries found new homes in Cleveland, too. Its variety of customs and religions has made Cleveland the most culturally diverse city in Ohio.

Asians and Pacific Islanders number about 91,000. People of Asian cultures trace their origins not only to China and Japan, but also to India, Korea, and the Philippines. Others are Vietnamese, Laotian, Cambodian, Thai, and Hmong. Ohio's Pacific Islanders include Hawaiians, Guamanians, and Samoans. About 1.3 percent of Ohioans are of Hispanic origin. Most originate from Mexico and Puerto Rico.

Attendees at the African-American Festival in Cleveland

The Long Road to Freedom

Before the Civil War, many Ohioans ignored the Fugitive Slave Law—which said that runaway slaves must be returned to their owners in the South—and risked their own security to help African-American slaves escape to freedom. From the Ohio River to Lake Erie, farmhouses and churches harbored escapees in secret cellars and attics.

Cincinnati 5-Way Chili

Cincinnati considers itself the chili capital of the world, and 5-way chili is a tradition. Legend has it that it was invented by Greek immigrants in the early 1900s. Named for its five major ingredients, this chili is served in chili parlors and diners all over southern Ohio.

Ingredients:

1 teaspoon salt

1 lb. ground chuck

2 onions, minced

2 garlic cloves, minced

1 cup tomato sauce

1 cup water

3 tablespoons barbecue sauce

1 tablespoon chili powder

1 teaspoon black pepper

1/2 oz. unsweetened grated chocolate

1/2 teaspoon ground cumin

1/2 teaspoon turmeric

1/2 teaspoon allspice

1/2 teaspoon cinnamon

1/4 teaspoon ground cloves

1/4 teaspoon ground coriander

1/4 teaspoon ground cardamom

9 oz. spaghetti, cooked

1 16-oz. can of red kidney beans, heated

2 onions, chopped

1 lb. shredded cheddar cheese

Directions:

Sprinkle salt in a large skillet and place over medium heat. Add beef, minced onions, and garlic. Stir until meat turns brown. Carefully drain the fat, then add tomato sauce, water, and barbecue sauce. Bring the mixture to a boil and add chili powder, pepper, chocolate, cumin, turmeric, allspice, cinnamon, cloves, coriander, and cardamom. Cover and simmer at lowest heat for 45 minutes, stirring occasionally. You may need to add more tomato sauce if the chili is getting too dry—but don't add too much.

While the chili is cooking, chop two onions, cook the spaghetti according to the directions on the package, and heat the kidney beans.

When everything is cooked, dish the spaghetti out onto dinner plates. Ladle a layer of chili on top of the noodles. Sprinkle some beans on top of the chili. Finally, cover it all with a layer of onions, then a generous layer of cheese. Use your hands to spread the cheese on each serving and pat it into place—you want the servings to look like tidy mounds.

Serves 4.

The African Methodist Episcopal (AME) Church played a major role in the Underground Railroad. Its circuit-riding ministers gathered information about safe houses and slave hunters. Even before slavery was abolished, the AME founded Wilberforce University to educate young members of the black community.

After the war, Ohio's African-American population began to grow. Only about 25,000 African-Americans lived in Ohio in 1850. But twenty years later, they numbered more than 63,000. Gradually they worked their way into Ohio's political, cultural, and economic life. John Mercer Langston of Oberlin was the country's first African-American elected to public office. Paul Laurence Dunbar of Dayton was the first African-American poet to become famous nationwide.

In the 1800s, most of Ohio's African-Americans lived in the southern part of the state. But as Ohio became more industrialized, its factories attracted thousands of African-Americans from other states. Between 1910 and 1930, Ohio's black population tripled, and the centers of population moved to the major cities. Today, African-Americans make up about 11 percent of Ohio's people. Novelist Toni Morrison, actress Ruby Dee, and many other African-American Ohioans continue to enrich the nation's cultural life.

Native Americans

About 20,000 Ohioans are Native Americans. In 1817, the last of Ohio's Indians—the Delaware, Seneca, and Wyandot—were assigned reservations in the northwest part of the state. One by one, even those lands were taken away. The Wyandot, in 1843, were the last to go.

Today, remnant groups of Ohio Indians hang on to their cultural identity, but they are not officially recognized by the U.S. government. They are the Ohio Band of the Allegheny Nation, the Shawnee Nation United Remnant Band, the Piqua Sept of Ohio Shawnees, and the Northeast Miami Inter-Tribal Council.

The Amish

Ohio is home to the largest community of Amish and Mennonite people in the world. They are spiritual descendants of Anabaptists, a Christian group that arose in Europe in the 1500s. In 1693, Jakob Ammann broke away from the others. He and his followers, known as the Amish, wanted a stricter lifestyle. About one-third of the 145,000 Amish who live in the United States and Canada today live in Ohio.

The Amish people live in farming communities covering about 400 square miles (1,036 sq km) of eastern Ohio. Wayne, Holmes, and Tuscarawas Counties are the heart of Amish country. These simple, devout people live according to the teachings of the Bible. Their beliefs rule out materialism and modern technology. Farm size is limited to the amount of land one family can manage without modern farm equipment.

Dancers at Sun Watch Indian Village

Life Among the Plain People

The Amish call themselves "the plain people." They take to heart the Bible passage that begins, "Be not conformed to the world" (Romans 12:2). For the Amish, this means wearing simple clothing and living apart from the modern world and popular culture. They believe in peaceful relations with others and practice nonviolence, even in the face of an attack.

Simplicity is more important than convenience. For example, the Amish travel in horse-drawn buggies instead of cars. Cars would speed up the pace of life and create a separation between wealthier and poorer members. However, an Amish person may accept a ride from a non-Amish driver.

Electricity, too, is considered worldly. The Amish see electric power lines as connections to the world that could lead to a breakdown in family life and religious devotion. No electricity means no television, radio, or electric lights.

Visitors to an Amish town may not notice at first that there is no electricity. Shops, restaurants, and homes are as brightly lit as any in the outside world because the use of natural-gas power is accepted. The Amish use tanks of bottled gas to operate their stoves, refrigerators, water heaters, lanterns, and lamps.

Amish men and boys dress in black trousers with suspenders and a black coat. They wear a broad-brimmed black hat, or, in the summer, a straw hat. Women and girls wear a long dress, and a bonnet or prayer cap. After an Amish man is married, he no longer shaves his beard.

All Amish settlements are rural farming communities—no one lives alone or in a city. Manual labor is valued highly, and the Amish make bread, cheese, jelly, furniture, quilts, comforters, and rugs by hand. November, after the autumn harvest, is the time for weddings. They take place on Tuesdays or Thursdays, the least-busy days of the week for the farmers.

Self-reliance and neighborly assistance are strong values among the Amish. They believe that if they are faithful to their religious values, their needs will be met. They do not expect the government to take care of them. For example, the Amish do not collect U.S. Social Security, Medicare, or Medicaid benefits. Instead, they take care of elderly and needy members within the family and the community. While they may seek modern medical care, they do not carry health insurance. Instead, they pay members' medical expenses out of a community fund. Members also pitch in to help their neighbors harvest crops and build houses and barns.

Children attend Amish schools through the eighth grade. After that, they continue a learning program supervised by their parents. In 1972, the U.S. Supreme Court ruled that Amish children do not have to follow state laws that require formal schooling after eighth grade. The Court pointed out that Amish communities are serious about giving their children an education. They object only to a type of education that could harm a child's religious development.

Amish customs and the Amish way of life may seem strict or even severe. But their rules of conduct are only for themselves. The Amish don't pass judgment on outsiders. Rather, they look on others with care, consideration, and loving kindness. ■

McGuffey's Readers

William H. McGuffey published his first readers in 1836 when he was president of Cincinnati College. McGuffey went on to become president of Ohio University (1839–1843) and a professor at the University of Virginia (1845–1873). He wrote seven readers in all. By 1920, more than 120 million copies had been sold.

McGuffey's readers not only taught reading, but they also conveyed a sense of good morals. noted American historian Henry Steele Commager commented that McGuffey's readers "gave to the American child of the nineteenth century what he so conspicuously lacks today—a common body of allusions, a sense of common experience and of common possession." McGuffey's home in Oxford is now a national historic landmark. ■

Schools

McGuffey's Eclectic Readers were the most common schoolbooks in the 1800s. From one-room wilderness schools to big-city classrooms, children learned to read with McGuffey's. In Ohio, teachers made sure their students knew that an Ohioan—William H. McGuffey—wrote the readers. Children learned how to spell from their "blue-backed spellers." First developed by Noah Webster in 1783, these blue-covered spelling books were used for over a hundred years.

David Zeisberger, a Moravian missionary, opened Ohio's first school in Schoenbrunn in 1773 to teach Indian children. Later, as pioneer settlements grew, children attended one-room schoolhouses made of logs. Sturdier schools were built in the early 1800s, as red-brick schoolhouses became the standard all over the state. By 1900, Ohio had 11,000 of these one-room schoolhouses.

In the early days, parents paid for their children's education. But a schoolteacher might have taken "tuition" in the form of wild game or baked goods. Churches often provided schools for their members' children. In 1825, the state began supporting public elementary schools. The first public high schools opened in 1853.

Today, children in Ohio must attend school between the ages of six and seventeen. Columbus was the first U.S. city to open a junior high school. Today, Indianola Middle School in Columbus proudly traces its history back to 1908.

The whole country's education system got a boost when Congress passed the Morrill Land Grant Act of 1862. It gave each state the right to sell huge tracts of public land to build colleges. That's how Ohio State University was established. OSU's main campus in Columbus is the largest campus in the country. Its Morrill Tower residence hall honors Justin Morrill, who authored the Land Grant Act.

Ohio University, the state's first public college, opened in Athens in 1804. Miami University, established in Oxford in 1809,

Ohio began supporting public elementary schools in 1825.

was the next to open. Oberlin College, a private school founded in 1833, was the first college in the country to admit both women and men. It was also one of the first to admit both black and white students. Other private colleges and universities in Ohio include Antioch College, Baldwin-Wallace College, Case Western Reserve University, and Denison University.

Opposite: Springtime at Miami University

CHAPTER TEN

Arts and Fun

What's the only state in the country that has a state rock song? Ohio! In 1985, the legislature named "Hang On Sloopy" to this glorious position. The McCoys, a rock band from Dayton, first recorded the tune in 1965, with hot guitar riffs by Celina-born Rick Derringer. "Sloopy" zoomed to the top of the national charts. Now the Ohio State University Marching Band plays its famous arrangement at football games.

State lawmakers didn't care if people thought "Sloopy" was a crazy idea—or if other music lovers felt left out. Their official resolution declared: "If fans of jazz, country-and-western, classical, Hawaiian, and polka music think those styles also should be recognized by the state, then by golly, they can push their own resolution just like we're doing."

If classical music fans decided to pick an official state orchestra, they'd probably name the Cleveland Orchestra. It's one of the greatest orchestras in the world, making frequent tours of Europe and Asia. It plays its regular season in Severance Hall, while the Blossom Music Center is its summer home. Among the orchestra's many famous conductors have been George Szell, Pierre Boulez, Lorin Maazel, and now Christoph von Dohnányi.

The Cincinnati Symphony Orchestra is also well known. Columbus, Toledo, and many other cities have their own orchestras,

Clark Gable was known for many roles on the silver screen.

Opposite: Having fun in Ohio

Lillian Gish

Doris Day

as well as opera and chamber music groups. Blossom Music Center, in Cuyahoga Falls south of Cleveland, holds a summer-long festival of classical, rock, pop, and jazz music.

The dashing actor Clark Gable was born in Cadiz, Ohio. He worked in the region's coal mines as a teen. Other Ohioans who made their mark on the silver screen are actresses Lillian Gish and Doris Day. Comedian Phyllis Diller is an Ohio native, too. Actress Dorothy Dandridge, born in Cleveland, was the first African-American woman to be nominated for an Academy Award after her appearance in *Carmen Jones* (1954).

Art

The Cleveland Museum of Art is one of the finest in the country. It's one of several museums within the city's University Circle. Cincinnati Museum Center is another multimuseum cultural center. Its art museum features art of all kinds—including costumes, American films, Persian rugs, musical instruments, and African art.

The Taft Museum, also in Cincinnati, was once the home of President Taft's brother Charles. Although it's a small museum, it contains fascinating collections of master paintings, ancient Chinese porcelains, and antique watches.

Toledo glass king Edward Libbey founded the Toledo Museum of Art. It displays not only paintings by the old masters but also a beautiful collection of art glass.

The Columbus Museum of Art was Ohio's first art museum. Its Howald Collection of early modern paintings is famous around the world. It also exhibits paintings by two Ohio artists—George Bellows and Elijah Pierce.

The Dairy Barn

Dairy cows used to mosey in for their daily milkings. Now art critics gather there to judge top-notch works of art. The Dairy Barn Southeastern Ohio Cultural Arts Center in Athens showcases the region's folk arts, crafts, and cultural heritage. Every two years, the Dairy Barn sponsors Quilt National, a show and competition featuring wildly creative quilts. The quilt artists include men and women from the United States and about twenty foreign countries. ■

Literary Ohioans

William Dean Howells (1837–1920), people said, could make or break an author by praising or panning a book. Howells was Ohio's first famous writer. He was highly respected as the editor of *Atlantic Monthly* magazine, where his book reviews appeared. Many of his own novels tell of his early years on the Ohio frontier.

Ambrose Bierce's (1842–1914?) writings had a sarcastic, hard-edged tone. *The Cynic's Word Book*—later published as *The Devil's Dictionary*—is Bierce's collection of pessimistic definitions. Some of his best works, however, were gripping Civil War stories.

Paul Laurence Dunbar (1872–1906) was the first African-American poet to rise to national fame. According to William Dean Howells, Dunbar was "the only man of pure African

The Cleveland Museum of Art houses one of the best art collections in the world. With more than 30,000 works of art, the museum can display only a small portion of them at one time. The oldest artifacts, from ancient Egypt and Asia, are more than 5,000 years old. Other pieces include medieval French tapestries and African religious objects. Some of the museum's most popular paintings are *Sunflower* by Georgia O'Keeffe, *After the Bath* by Mary Cassatt, *Water Lilies* by Claude Monet, and *Still Life with Biscuits* by Pablo Picasso. Children's programs include art classes, hands-on workshops, and a Chalk Festival. ■

Maya's Wall

Maya Ying Lin (1960–) of Athens designed the Vietnam Veterans Memorial that stands in Washington, D.C. Her design was chosen from more than 1,500 submissions. At the time, Lin was a twenty-one-year-old architecture student at Yale University. Etched on two black granite walls are the names of 58,000 Americans who were killed in the Vietnam War or who were still missing in 1982 when the memorial was built. It stands on the capital's National Mall, and many of the millions of visitors leave notes, medals, and flowers in honor of their loved ones. ■

blood . . . to feel the Negro life aesthetically and express it lyrically." *Oak and Ivy*, his first published poetry collection, was widely acclaimed. At the time it was published in 1893, Dunbar was working as an elevator operator in Dayton.

Dunbar wrote most of his poetry in black dialect. In time, he felt "trapped" in the dialect and wished that critics would recognize his works in standard English. But he was so well known as a black spokesperson that it was hard to change people's expectations. Dunbar's Dayton home, with the book-filled study where he wrote, is an Ohio state memorial.

Novelist Harriet Beecher Stowe (1811–1896) lived in Cincinnati for eighteen years. From her home along the Ohio River, she heard many tales of slaves who escaped to freedom. One dramatic incident involved a young slave girl who floated to freedom on the river's icy floes. Stowe later retold the harrowing scene with her character Eliza in *Uncle Tom's Cabin*.

William Sydney Porter used the pen name O. Henry in his charming and zany short stories. "The Gift of the Magi" and "The Ransom of Red Chief" are two of his favorite tales. Porter was

Harriet Beecher Stowe, author of *Uncle Tom's Cabin*

not an Ohio native, but he spent some time in the Ohio State Penitentiary!

Sherwood Anderson (1876–1941) wrote tales of small-town America. He's best known for his novel *Winesburg, Ohio.* Poet Hart Crane (1899–1932) made his mark with two volumes of poetry.

Zanesville was the hometown of Zane Grey (1875–1939). His

James Thurber

Humorist and cartoonist James Thurber (1894–1961) was one of the funniest people ever. He liked to show how ridiculous and frustrating life can be. *The Owl in the Attic and Other Perplexities* and *The Seal in the Bedroom and Other Predicaments* are some of his early collections. His children's books include *The Thirteen Clocks*. Dogs were among his favorite cartoon subjects. Born in Columbus, Thurber contributed cartoons and stories to *The New Yorker* magazine from 1927 until his death. He once declared, "Sixty minutes of thinking of any kind is bound to lead to confusion and unhappiness." ■

Western novels created our popular image of the American West as a rugged but romantic scene. *Riders of the Purple Sage* is Gray's best-known novel.

Hilarious cartoons and stories streamed from the pen of James Thurber (1894–1961). Fans were likely to see his work first in *The New Yorker* magazine. Thurber's home in Columbus, now a museum and literary center, pops up frequently in *My Life and Hard Times.*

Today, several Ohio women have reached the top of their fields in the literary world. Toni Morrison of Lorain is a Nobel Prize–winning novelist. Poet Rita Dove of Akron was named the United States Poet Laureate.

Professional and College Sports

Ohio is one of the great states for major-league sports. Seven major-league professional teams make their home in Ohio: baseball's Cincinnati Reds and Cleveland Indians; football's Cincinnati Bengals and Cleveland Browns; basketball's Cleveland Cavaliers; hockey's Columbus Blue Jackets; and women's basketball's team the Cleveland Rockers.

Zane Grey was known for his Western novels.

Major-league baseball history has it origins in Ohio. The National League was created in 1869 with the formation of the Cincinnati Red Stockings (now called the Reds), the world's first professional baseball team. The Reds' illustrious history has featured many World Series champions, but perhaps the greatest team of all was the "Big Red Machine" of the the 1970s. Winners of the 1975 and 1976 World Series, these Reds featured such great players as Pete Rose, Joe Morgan, and Johnny Bench. Morgan and Bench are in Baseball's Hall of Fame, but Rose is not.

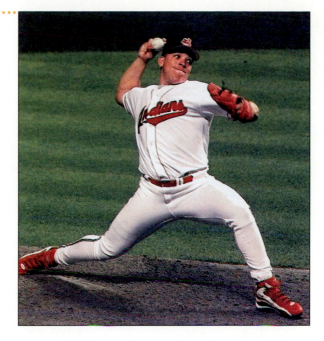

Cleveland Indians pitcher Bartolo Colon in the 1998 American League championship series against the New York Yankees

Rose was born in Cincinnati, and in his playing career he became the city's greatest hero. Nicknamed Charlie Hustle for his hard-nosed playing style, he collected more hits—4,256—than any player in history. But his career and life were marred in 1989 when he was banned from baseball for life for gambling on Reds games while he was the team's manager. In recent years, Rose has tried to win back his Hall of Fame eligibility.

The Cleveland Indians have represented Ohio in the American League since 1915. In 1947, the Indians hired Larry Doby, making him the first African-American in the American League (following Jackie Robinson, who had broken the color barrier in the National League). Indians fans are long-suffering—the team hasn't won the World Series since Doby led them to the championship in 1948. In the 1970s, the Indians played so poorly that distraught fans nicknamed them the Mistake by the Lake. But things changed in the

Say It Ain't So, Joe!

Joseph Jefferson "Shoeless Joe" Jackson (1887–1951) was one of baseball's greatest hitters. His lifetime batting average of .356 is the third highest in major-league history. Jackson got his nickname as a minor-leaguer. His new spikes hurt his feet so badly that he took to the field in his stocking feet. Later, Jackson was an outfielder for the Cleveland Indians (1910–1915) and the Chicago White Sox (1915–1920). His career was cut short after the "Black Sox" scandal. He and seven other White Sox were accused of accepting bribes to lose the 1919 World Series to the Cincinnati Reds. Although a jury acquitted Jackson, he was banned from baseball and barred forever from the Baseball Hall of Fame. According to legend, a boy shouted through the crowd as Jackson left the courtroom, "Say it ain't so, Joe!" ■

1990s. Their spectacular new ball park, Jacobs Field (opened in 1994), is considered the centerpiece of downtown Cleveland's revival. And ever since moving to "the Jake," the team has played well, too!

Ohio also plays a key role in the history of professional football. The National Football League (NFL) was organized in Canton in 1920. Now Canton is home to the National Professional Football Hall of Fame. The original Cleveland Browns were one of the legendary NFL teams for many decades. Named for Paul Brown, their first-ever head coach, the team won four championships, the last in 1964. But in 1996, the team moved east and became the Baltimore Ravens. In 1999, a new franchise using the much-loved Browns name started play in a newly constructed Browns Stadium.

Outside of Ohio, people might not know that Paul Brown had links to many football institutions besides the Cleveland Browns. After his historic career with Cleveland, Brown founded—and

Frank Robinson

A Baseball Hall of Famer who made his mark with both Ohio teams was the great slugger Frank Robinson. Robinson broke into the big leagues with the Cincinnati Reds in 1956 and went on to hit 586 home runs in his career (only three men have hit more). In 1975, Robinson made history when he was named player-manager of the Cleveland Indians, becoming the first African-American manager in major-league history. ■

Jim Brown

One of the most intense and dedicated American athletes ever, Jim Brown played for the Cleveland Browns from 1957 to 1965. Brown was inducted into the Pro Football Hall of Fame in 1971. In his post-playing years, Brown has been an outspoken critic of modern athletes for their failure to be good role models for young people, and he is active in numerous civil rights activities. ■

was the first coach of—the Cincinnati Bengals in 1969. When it opens in 2000, the Bengals' new playing facility will be named Paul Brown Stadium. Before he joined the Browns in 1946, Paul had been a head coach at Ohio State University, leading the Buckeyes to a national football championship in 1942. In the years since, Ohio State has remained a force in college athletics.

OSU's greatest student-athlete was also one of the great Americans of the twentieth century—Jesse Owens. Owens spent much of his childhood in Cleveland and enrolled at Ohio State in 1933. Breaking just about every college track-and-field record imaginable, the "Buckeye Bullet" quickly became the most famous athlete in the nation. He then rose to worldwide acclaim when he went to Berlin, Germany, for the 1936 Olympic Games. He embarrassed Adolf Hilter by leading an American sweep of the track-and-field events. Hitler had hoped to use the Olympics to prove the superiority of white Aryans, but the African-American Owens defeated every challenger and won four gold medals.

Celebrating Ohio Life

Ohioans find plenty of ways to celebrate their heritage, their work, and their daily life. Troy holds its annual Strawberry Festival in

The Strawberry Festival parade

June. Meanwhile, Cincinnati hosts Summerfair, an arts and crafts festival with plenty of food and entertainment.

Loudonville is the site of the Great Mohican Indian Pow-Wow every summer. Native Americans of many tribes attend to celebrate their culture with foods, crafts, storytelling, and dancing. The Indian Summer Festival in Wapakoneta honors the city's Native American heritage with a parade, craft show, and children's activities.

In August, thousands of twins from all over the world gather for the Twins Day Festival in Twinsburg. With more than 3,000 sets of twins, triplets, and quadruplets attending, the festival has made it into *The Guiness Book of World Records*.

Historic Sauder Village is full of delicious aromas in September. That's when huge copper kettles bubble and boil with apple butter, made the old-fashioned way. Lima's Apple Festival features not only apple butter making, but also an apple-pie contest, sugarcorn popped over an open fire, and a straw maze for kids. Zoar, Elyria, Holland, Belpre, Gnadenhutten, Burton, and Oak Harbor have apple butter festivals, too.

Oxford's Ohio Honey Festival in September celebrates beekeeping and honey production. It also features a contest for the best beehive hairdo. October brings Octoberfests and countless other harvest festivals.

The National Afro-American Museum and Cultural Center in Wilberforce is the scene of year-round cultural events. In October, it presents a Holiday Festival of Black Dolls from around the country. The traditional Kwanzaa festival is December's highlight.

Hikers bundle up for a fascinating journey in Waynesville's Winter Hike. They trek past frozen waterfalls and towering cliffs draped with huge icicles and wobble across a swinging cable bridge.

March is the time when Ohioans collect maple tree sap and boil it down to make maple syrup. At the Maple Syrup Festival in Waverly, visitors can watch how the syrup is made—and, of course, taste the results. Other syrup sites are the Brukner Nature Center in Troy, Paint Creek State Park in Hillsboro, and Aurora Farms in Aurora.

These are just a few of the ways Ohioans celebrate their diversity and share their warmth with neighbors near and far.

The Twins Day Festival is just one event that celebrates life in Ohio.

Timeline

United States History

1607 The first permanent English settlement is established in North America at Jamestown.

1620 Pilgrims found Plymouth Colony, the second permanent English settlement.

1776 America declares its independence from Britain.

1783 The Treaty of Paris officially ends the Revolutionary War in America.

1787 The U.S. Constitution is written.

1803 The Louisiana Purchase almost doubles the size of the United States.

1812–15 The United States and Britain fight the War of 1812.

Ohio State History

c. 1670 The French explorer René-Robert Cavelier, Sieur de La Salle, is believed to be the first European to reach what is today Ohio.

1763 France surrenders its claim to the Ohio region to Britain.

1786 The Ohio Company is organized in Virginia to colonize the Ohio River valley.

1787 The U.S. Congress establishes the Northwest Territory.

1788 Marietta becomes the first permanent European settlement in Ohio.

1795 The Treaty of Greenville ends the Indian wars in the Ohio region.

1800 The Division Act divides the Northwest Territory into two parts; Chillicothe is named the capital of the territory called Ohio.

1803 On March 1, Ohio becomes the seventeenth state.

1813 Commodore Oliver H. Perry's fleet defeats the British in the Battle of Lake Erie.

United States History

The North and South fight **1861–65** each other in the American Civil War.

The United States is **1917–18** involved in World War I.

The stock market crashes, **1929** plunging the United States into the Great Depression.

The United States **1941–45** fights in World War II.
The United States becomes a **1945** charter member of the U.N.

The United States **1951–53** fights in the Korean War.

The U.S. Congress enacts a series of **1964** groundbreaking civil rights laws.

The United States **1964–73** engages in the Vietnam War.

The United States and other **1991** nations fight the brief Persian Gulf War against Iraq.

Ohio State History

1832 The Ohio and Erie Canal is completed.

1845 The Miami and Erie Canal is completed.

1870 Benjamin F. Goodrich opens a rubber goods plant in Akron.

1914 Ohio passes the Conservancy Act after floods in 1913.

1922 The Miami River valley flood-control project is finished.

1938 The flood-control project in the Muskingum River valley is completed.

1955 The Ohio Turnpike opens for truck and automobile traffic.

1959 The terms of the governor and other high state officials are increased from two years to four.

1967 Ohio voters approve a plan to reapportion the state legislature.

1971 Ohio adopts an income tax.

1993 Ohio voters approve the sale of $200 million worth of bonds to finance improvements and expansion in the state's parks and other recreation areas.

Fast Facts

Capitol

Statehood date	March 1, 1803, the 17th state
Origin of state name	From the Seneca word for "beautiful river"
State capital	Columbus
State nickname	Buckeye State
State motto	"With God, All Things Are Possible"
State bird	Cardinal
State flower	Scarlet carnation
State wildflower	White trillium
State fish	Walleye
State insect	Ladybug
State animal	White-tailed deer
State reptile	Black racer snake
State fossil	Trilobite
State gemstone	Ohio flint
State beverage	Tomato juice
State song	"Beautiful Ohio"

Ladybug

Ohio River

State tree	Ohio buckeye
State fair	Mid-August at Columbus
Total area; rank	44,828 sq. mi. (116,105 sq km); 35th
Land; rank	40,953 sq. mi. (106,068 sq km); 35th
Water; rank	3,875 sq. mi. (10,036 sq km); 11th
Inland water; rank	376 sq. mi. (974 sq km); 37th
Great Lakes; rank	3,499 sq. mi. (9,062 sq km); 4th
Geographic center	Delaware, 25 miles (40 km) north-northeast of Columbus
Latitude and longitude	Ohio is located approximately between 38° 27' and 41° 57' N and 80° 34' and 84° 49' W
Highest point	Campbell Hill, 1,550 feet (472 m)
Lowest point	Ohio River, 433 feet (132 m)
Largest city	Columbus
Number of counties	88
Population; rank	10,887,325 (1990 census); 7th
Density	263 persons per sq. mi. (102 per sq km)
Population distribution	74% urban, 26% rural

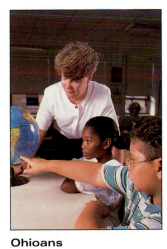

Ohioans

Ethnic distribution (does not equal 100%)

White	87.78%
African-American	10.65%
Hispanic	1.29%
Asian and Pacific Islanders	0.84%
Other	0.54%
Native American	0.19%

Record high temperature	113°F (45°C) near Gallipolis on July 21, 1934

Coneflowers and black-eyed Susans

Record low temperature	−39°F (−39 °C) at Milligan on February 10, 1899
Average July temperature	73°F (23°C)
Average January temperature	28°F (−2°C)
Average annual precipitation	38 inches (97 cm)

Natural Areas and Historic Sites

National Recreation Area

Cuyahoga Valley National Recreation Area preserves the natural areas of the valley between Akron and Cleveland.

National Historical Parks

Dayton Aviation Heritage National Historical Park honors the achievements of the area's aviation pioneers—Wilbur and Orville Wright. The park also honors the life and work of African-American poet Paul Laurence Dunbar.

Hopewell Culture National Historical Park displays artifacts from the Hopewell Culture (100 B.C. to A.D. 500) and burial mounds.

National Historic Sites

James A. Garfield National Historic Site contains properties associated with the twentieth president of the United States.

William Howard Taft National Historic Site is the birthplace and boyhood home of the twenty-seventh president of the United States and the tenth chief justice of the Supreme Court.

National Memorial

Perry's Victory and International Peace Memorial commemorates the peace between the United States and Canada near the site of a U.S. victory in the War of 1812.

Orville and Wilbur Wright

**Old Man's Cave
State Park**

National Forests

Wayne National Forest is in southern and southeastern Ohio.

State Parks

Ohio has nine state parks, the largest of which is Shawnee-Roosevelt State Forest.

Sports Teams

NCAA Teams (Division 1)

Bowling Green State University Falcons

Cleveland State University Vikings

Kent State University Golden Flashes

Miami University Redskins

Ohio State University Buckeyes

Ohio University Bobcats

University of Akron Zips

University of Cincinnati Bearcats

University of Dayton Flyers

University of Toledo Rockets

Wright State University Raiders

Xavier University Musketeers

Youngstown State University Penguins

Major League Baseball

Cincinnati Reds

Cleveland Indians

National Basketball Association

Cleveland Cavaliers

National Football League

Cincinnati Bengals

Cleveland Browns

Bartolo Colon

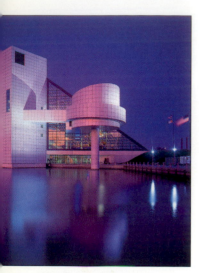

**Rock and Roll
Hall of Fame**

National Hockey League
Columbus Blue Jackets

Women's National Basketball Association
Cleveland Rockers

Major League Soccer
Columbus Crew

Cultural Institutions

Libraries

Cleveland, Columbus, Cincinnati, Toledo, Dayton, and Youngstown all have outstanding public libraries.

Cincinnati Historical Society, *Martha Kinney Cooper Ohioana Library* (Columbus), and the *Archive of Ohio Folklore* (Miami University) all have fine collections on Ohio history.

Museums

Ohio Historical Center (Columbus) has extensive collections and exhibits devoted to Ohio's archaeology, history, and wildlife.

Ohio has many wonderful art museums, including the *Cincinnati Art Museum*, the *Taft Museum* (Cincinnati), the *Columbus Museum of Art*, the *Cleveland Museum of Art,* the *Dayton Art Institute,* and the *Toledo Museum of Art.* All of these contain fine collections of paintings, sculpture, and other artworks from around the world.

Performing Arts

Ohio has six major opera companies, six major symphony orchestras, and seven major dance companies.

Universities and Colleges

In the mid-1990s, Ohio had sixty-one public and ninety-five private institutions of higher learning.

Miami University

Strawberry Festival

Annual Events

January–March
Ohio Winter Ski Carnival in Mansfield (February)

Buzzard Day in Hinckley (March)

Maple Syrup Festival in Waverly (March)

American-Canadian Sport Show in Cleveland (March)

April–June
Geauga County Maple Festival in Chardon (April)

Appalachian Festival in Cincinnati (May)

Walleye Festival in Port Clinton (May)

Festival of the Fish in Vermilion (June)

Cherry Festival in Bellevue (June)

Ports and Maritime Festival in Cleveland (June)

Memorial Golf Tournament in Dublin (June)

Strawberry Festival in Troy (June)

July–September
Budweiser Cleveland Grand Prix in Cleveland (July)

Dayton Air Show in Vandalia (July)

Jamboree in the Hills in Morristown (July)

Pro Football Hall of Fame Festival in Canton (July)

Ohio State Fair in Columbus (August)

Salt Fork Arts & Crafts Festival in Cambridge (August)

Twins Day Festival in Twinsburg (August)

Ohio River Sternwheel Festival in Marietta (September)

Riverfest in Cincinnati (September)

Grape Jamboree in Geneva (September)

Twins Day Festival

October–December

Bob Evans Farm Festival in Rio Grande (October)

Paul Bunyan Show in Nelsonville (October)

Apple Butter Stirrin' in Coshocton (October)

Pumpkin Show in Circleville (October)

Winterfest at Kings Island near Cincinnati (December)

Christmas at Ohio Village in Columbus (December)

Christmas Candlelightings in Coshocton (December)

Famous People

Sherwood Anderson (1876–1941)	Author
Neil Alden Armstrong (1930–)	Astronaut
George Armstrong Custer (1839–1876)	Soldier
Doris Day (1924–)	Actor
Thomas Alva Edison (1847–1931)	Inventor
Clark Gable (1901–1960)	Actor
James Abram Garfield (1831–1881)	U.S. president
Lillian Gish (1893–1993)	Actor
John Herschel Glenn Jr. (1921–)	Astronaut and senator
Ulysses S. Grant (1822–1885)	U.S. president
Zane Grey (1875–1939)	Author
Warren Gamaliel Harding (1865–1923)	U.S. president
Benjamin Harrison (1833–1901)	U. S. president
Rutherford Birchard Hayes (1822–1893)	U.S. president
William McKinley (1843–1901)	U. S. president
Toni Morrison (1931–)	Author
Paul Newman (1925–)	Actor
Jack William Nicklaus (1940–)	Golfer

John Glenn

Thomas Edison

Annie Oakley (1860–1926)	Sharpshooter
Pontiac (1720?–1769)	American Indian leader
Edward Vernon Rickenbacker (1890–1973)	Aviator and businessperson
Philip Henry Sheridan (1831–1888)	Soldier
William Tecumseh Sherman (1820–1891)	Soldier
Steven Spielberg (1947–)	Film director
Harriet Beecher Stowe (1811–1896)	Author
Robert Alphonso Taft (1889–1953)	Public official
William Howard Taft (1857–1930)	U.S. president
James Grover Thurber (1894–1961)	Humorist and cartoonist

James Thurber

To Find Out More

History

- Brown, Dottie. *Ohio.* Minneapolis: Lerner, 1992.

- Cavan, Seamus. *Daniel Boone and the Opening of the Ohio Country*. Broomall, Penn.: Chelsea House, 1991.

- Chambers, Catherine E. *Flatboats on the Ohio: Westward Bound*. Mahwah, N.J.: Troll, 1998.

- Fradin, Dennis Brindell. *Ohio.* Chicago: Childrens Press, 1993.

- Hiscock, Bruce. *The Big Rivers: The Missouri, the Mississippi, and the Ohio*. New York: Atheneum, 1997.

- Peacock, Nancy. *Kidding Around Cleveland: A Fun Filled, Fact Packed Travel & Activity Book*. Santa Fe, N.M.: John Muir Publications, 1997.

- Thompson, Kathleen. *Ohio.* Austin, Tex.: Raintree/Steck Vaughn, 1996.

- Wills, Charles A. *A Historical Album of Ohio*. Brookfield, Conn.: Millbrook, 1996.

Fiction

- Holbrook, Sara. *What's So Big about Cleveland, Ohio?* Cleveland: Gray & Co., 1997.

- Willis, Patricia. *Danger Along the Ohio*. New York: Clarion Books, 1997.

Biographies

- Collins, David R. *Johnny Appleseed: God's Faithful Planter, John Chapman*. New York: Fromm International, 1986.

- Gentry, Tony. *Paul Laurence Dunbar*. Broomall, Penn.: Chelsea House, 1989.

- Kent, Zachary. *William McKinley*. Chicago: Childrens Press, 1988.

- Kramer, Barbara. *John Glenn: A Space Biography*. Springfield, N.J.: Enslow, 1998.

Websites

- **State of Ohio**
  http://www.state.oh.us
  The official website of Ohio with links to a variety of state agencies and departments

Addresses

- **Ohio Division of Travel and Tourism**
  P.O. Box 1001
  Columbus, OH 43266-0001
  For information on tourism in Ohio

- **Department of Development**
  State Office Tower II
  77 South High Street
  Columbus, OH 43215
  For information on the Ohio economy

- **Secretary of State**
  30 East Broad Street
  14th Floor
  Columbus, OH 43266
  For information about Ohio government

- **Ohio Historical Center Educational Services Department**
  1985 Velma Avenue
  Columbus, OH 43211
  For information about Ohio history

Index

Page numbers in *italics* indicate illustrations.

Meet the Author

Ann Heinrichs fell in love with faraway places while reading Doctor Dolittle books as a child. She has traveled through most of the United States and several countries in Europe, as well as northwest Africa, the Middle East, and east Asia. Visits to Ohio have taken her through forests, across plains, and up and down the precipitous Cincinnati hills.

"Trips are fun, but the real work—tracking down all the factual information for a book—begins at the library. I head straight for the reference department. Some of my favorite resources are statistical abstracts and the library's computer databases.

"For this book, I also read local newspapers from several Ohio cities. The internet was a super research tool, too. The state library and various state agencies have websites that are chock full of information.

"To me, writing nonfiction is a bigger challenge than writing fiction. With nonfiction, you can't just dream something up—everything has to be researched. When I uncover the facts, they always turn out to be more spectacular than fiction could ever be."

Ann Heinrichs grew up in Fort Smith, Arkansas, and now lives in Chicago. She is the author of more than thirty books for children and young adults on American, Asian, and African history and culture. Several of her books have received state and national awards.

Ms. Heinrichs has also written numerous newspaper, magazine, and encyclopedia articles and critical reviews. As an advertising copywriter, she has covered everything from plumbing hardware to Oriental rugs and porcelain dolls. She holds a bachelor's and master's degree in piano performance. These days, her performing arts are t'ai chi chuan and kung fu sword.

Photo Credits

Photographs ©:

AP/Wide World Photos: 34 bottom, 130 bottom (Courtesy of the National Air and Space Museum, Smithsonian Institution), 121, 131 bottom (Tony Dejak), 84 top (Chris Kasson), 84 bottom, 134 top (David J. Phillip), 116 bottom
Corbis-Bettmann: 36, 38, 39, 98, 99, 118 top, 120, 122, 135 (UPI), 25, 29 bottom, 30, 33, 37, 72 bottom, 83, 110, 115, 134 bottom
Dembinsky Photo Assoc.: 46 top (Sharon Cummings), 78 bottom (John Gerlach), 46 bottom (Adam Jones), 6 bottom, 79, 128 bottom (Ed Kanze)
Envision: 105 (Steven Needham)
Gamma-Liaison, Inc.: 119 (U. Andersen), 35 (Hulton Getty), 116 top (Roger-Viollet)
Ian Adams Photography: 6 top left, 6 top center, 7 bottom, 32, 43, 47, 48, 60, 64, 69, 74, 78 top, 89, 112, 113, 130 top, 132 bottom
New England Stock Photo: 62, 73 (Roger Bickel), 56 (Jean Higgins)
North Wind Picture Archives: 13, 16 top, 18, 20, 21, 24, 91 top

Ohio Division of Travel and Tourism: 10
Photri: 88
Randall L. Schieber: 7 top center, 8, 26, 45, 51, 67, 77, 80, 108, 117, 129 top, 132 top
Stock Montage, Inc.: 12, 16 bottom, 19, 23, 27, 28, 29 top, 31, 34 top, 57, 72 top, 118 bottom
Superstock, Inc.: 92
The Hoover Company, North Canton, Ohio: 91 bottom
The Image Finders: 54, 63, 65, 87, 101, 104 (Jim Baron), 94 (Rita Byron), 100 (Janet Cobb), 7 top right, 97 (Michael Evans), 111, 129 bottom (Neil A. Gloger), 55, 76, 128 top (William A. Holmes), 114 (Novastock), 125, 133 bottom (Scott Pease), 53 (John Petrus), cover (Carl A. Stimac), 2, 107, 124, 133 top (Jim Yokajty)
Tom Till: 6 top right, 14, 42, 49, 131 top
Tony Stone Images: 7 top left, 58 (Peter Pearson), back cover (Donovan Reese)
Unicorn Stock Photos: 9, 71 (Jean Higgins)
Maps by XNR Productions, Inc.